FAMILY SPORTS ADVENTURES

EXCITING VACATIONS FOR PARENTS & KIDS TO SHARE

By MEGAN STINE

A *Sports Illustrated For Kids* Book

First Edition

Library of Congress Cataloging-in-Publication Data

Stine, Megan.
    Family sports adventures : exciting vacations for
parents and kids to share / Megan Stine.— 1st ed.
        p.   cm.
    "A Sports illustrated for kids book."
    ISBN 0-316-81626-4
    1. Sports camps—United States—Guide-books.   2. Camps—United
States—Guide-books.   3. Family recreation—United States—Guide-
books.   4. United States—Description and travel—1981–   —Guide-
books.   I. Title.
GV583.S85   1991
796'.071'073—dc20   90-49764

SPORTS ILLUSTRATED FOR KIDS is a trademark of
THE TIME INC. MAGAZINE COMPANY.

Sports Illustrated For Kids Books is a joint imprint of Little, Brown and
Company and Warner Juvenile Books. This title is published in
arrangement with Cloverdale Press Inc.

10 9 8 7 6 5 4 3 2 1

BP

For further information regarding this title, write to Little, Brown and
Company, 34 Beacon Street, Boston, MA 02108

Published simultaneously in Canada by Little, Brown & Company
(Canada) Limited

Printed in the United States of America

Interior Illustrations by Jennifer Bevill

CONTENTS

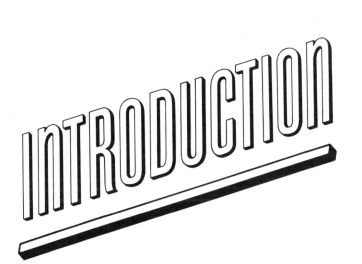

envy you. You are about to begin an adventure that I have just completed, the adventure of discovering how many fascinating sports-oriented escapes are possible. You'll be dazzled by visions of athletic odysseys and sports pilgrimages, of fabulous family expeditions that will take you to places you never knew existed. In some ways, this time of discovery and anticipation may be the most exciting for you and your family, because it's a time when vacation skies promise to be sunny and everyone is sure to love the food at every meal. But even reality won't mar the pleasure that's inherent in these adventures. When it rains on a sailing trip or the snow melts on the ski slopes, you'll still come home with the feeling that you've done something wonderful, something new and different and rejuvenating, that in some small way has changed your life.

What exactly is an adventure in sports? In this book, the sports adventures run the gamut from a wilderness trip at 8,000 feet above sea level to a visit to the Olympic Training Center in Colorado Springs, to a fan's-eye view of pro football training camps. There are adventures for people who want to do and try everything—skiing, hot air ballooning, cross-country bicycling, horseback riding, and more. And there are adventures for people who would rather watch sports and learn about sports than actually participate. Football, baseball, basketball, hockey, and many of the Olympic sports are represented, with inside tips about how you and your kids can see the players in less structured settings and maybe even rub elbows with a few stars.

But hey, you may be saying, with three young kids, we can't afford to take our family to a dude ranch or a ski resort. Relax. This book isn't just about expensive week-long vacations that have been planned months in advance. Sure, some of those are described, but there are also plenty of sports adventures you can have on relatively short notice, or on a tight budget. Perhaps your kids are sick to death of the school/home/friends routine and they need to get away from it all in the middle of a bleak winter. Or maybe you've already made summer vacation plans that aren't particularly thrilling: You're off to visit Grandma again, for example.

What you need in either case is a little excitement—something to spice up the familiar routine. Maybe a weekend of cross-country skiing will dissolve the mid-winter blues. A one-day whitewater rafting trip tacked onto the beginning or end of the trip could enliven the visit to Grandma. Those out of the ordinary breaks from everyday life can make all the difference in your family's mental health—and they make memories that will last a lifetime, as well.

Speaking of Grandma, don't forget that "family" adventures can include any collection of children and adults who want to enjoy a vacation together. Single parents, grandparents, aunts and uncles, and groups of good friends can all participate in these adventures together. Whitewater rafting, for example, is a great adventure for a larger group of family members or friends because the outing often requires a minimum number of participants anyway. Extend your family whenever possible, and you'll find that the adventurous spirit is infectious.

Whatever your time frame, whatever your family configuration, whatever your budget, you'll find an adventure here to suit your needs.

A few words about the book's organization and approach: Each sport has been described for the benefit of the beginner, with an emphasis on equipment, locales, and strategies that will make the sport easier and more enjoyable the first time out. So if you're an expert skier, you may not get much out of the section on skiing. Similarly, if you've canoed on the Colorado River in the spring, you'll undoubtedly be bored with the flat water canoe trips offered in the chapter on Water Sports Adventures, page 101. But few people are experts in every sport, and chances are that you'll find plenty of other adventures in the book worthy of your investigation. Also, families who are teetering on the brink of trying a new sport or activity can rest assured that all these activities are within reach of anyone who is in good health and reasonably fit condition. In a few cases, some pre-adventure conditioning is recommended, but we're not suggesting marathon workouts, just sensible preparation to insure that you'll get maximum enjoyment (and minimum muscle soreness) from your trip.

One other note regarding the skiing section in Wide Open Spaces: You'll find that there are no recommendations for particular ski lodges, ski schools, equipment outfitters, meals, or lodging. Instead, ski resort *areas* are recommended, with phone numbers and addresses listed to contact for more specific information. The reason for this is simple: People usually select a skiing destination based on the characteristics of the mountain itself, rather than on an individual ski lodge or other auxiliary facilities on that mountain. Each resort area offers a variety of accommodations—too many and too different to list in a book of this scope. Fortunately, the ski resort areas themselves will provide ample information to help you make good choices about accommodations.

As for the price rates quoted in this book: They are accurate as of mid-1990, but as you know, rates tend to go up. The first thing you should do when you're interested in a particular sports vacation is to write or call and ask for brochures. There are brochures available for *everything*—and poring over them can become an enjoyable family activity in itself. Rates and particulars are updated each year; be sure to read the brochures carefully for minimum age requirements, cancellation policies, and descriptions of what is included in the package rate.

So, welcome to the first of many adventures! Read on to discover how an average family, even a family of not particularly athletic people, can become involved in a wide range of sports experiences, and have a fantastic time doing it!

How to Make
Sure Your
Family Has Fun

Great vacations begin at home.

Put another way, successful vacations don't "just happen" through a series of lucky accidents. They succeed because of careful planning and consideration for each family member's wishes and needs. When you plan your vacation with care, taking into consideration your own interests and your children's—being realistic, and following the third and most important rule of vacation management by making copious lists—you're bound to have at least a moderately enjoyable trip. And it's much more likely that your vacation will take off like a Roman candle on the Fourth of July.

This chapter is about great planning strategies. It's full of tips, checklists and reminders of the best techniques for traveling with children.

CHOOSING YOUR OWN ADVENTURE

First of all, you have the delightful task of choosing a family sports adventure that everyone will enjoy. And that's the first hot tip for this chapter: *Choose a sport everyone will enjoy.* It's not going to be much fun to go tearing off on a four-day bicycle tour if your child is too young to pedal six or more miles per day. And if your spouse hates water sports, you really shouldn't push for a rafting trip, no matter how much everyone else wants to do it. Of course, it's always possible to put together a non-traditional family of one parent, an uncle and one kid from each family unit, for instance. That's a great way to experience some of the sports adventures that don't appeal to everyone in your household. But when you're planning a trip for the people you live with most of the time, you'll do *everyone* (including yourself) a favor if you take everyone's interests into account.

The biggest pitfall, one you should always try to avoid, is pushing a younger child into a situation he or she isn't ready for yet. Let's say you have a family of two parents, a 12-year-old, a 9-year-old and a toddler. Maybe four of you are desperate to go backpacking through the Sierra Mountains. No one needs to tell you that the toddler won't have or *be* much fun on this trek. In fact, he or she won't be able to keep up at all. So why not wait a few years for that trip, and try a dude ranch vacation this year instead? At many dude ranches and other sports-vacation resorts you'll find a children's program for little ones, and enough of the great outdoors to satisfy the wanderlust in the rest of the family members. In other words, adapt your expectations to the reality of your children's ages and abilities.

On the other hand, there's no reason to postpone a trip to the Baseball Hall of Fame just because one child is too young to read the plaques. Go ahead with that trip—just make sure you arrange to spend some time inside the museum, and some time outside letting your toddler run around.

A great way to be sure you're choosing the right vacation, and a great way to get your kids psyched for the trip, is to involve them in the decision-making from the start. Give them the brochures you've collected, let them pick and choose their favorites and then have a family meeting to discuss the options. But this doesn't mean you have to let your children make the decision for you. Family meetings work best when they are structured as discussion times rather than decision times. Listen to what each person has to say, then make your decision privately. Your kids will feel good just knowing that you took their opinions into account when the vacation was being planned.

One last tip about choosing a sports adventure: Read the brochures carefully. I've said this before and I'll say it again, because it's very easy to miss a key point amidst all the appealing color photographs and glowing descriptions. Don't assume that if *most* ski resorts have a childcare program, *all* of them have childcare. Or that all the raft trips offered by one outfitter include meals. Or that a canoeing trip will be cancelled if it's raining, thundering and lightning that day. Always read the fine print carefully.

HOW TO INTRODUCE YOUR CHILDREN TO A NEW SPORT

Put yourself in your child's place. How would you feel if someone told you that, whether you wanted to or not, you were going to skydive out of an airplane tomorrow afternoon? And moreover, you were expected to like it, and to thank them for the great opportunity.

That's how many children feel about having new experiences foisted upon them, especially if the experience requires some level of skill, courage or physical prowess. If your child is the jump-in-with-both-feet-type, you can skip these next few words of advice. But most of us need to prepare our children for new experiences with care and sensitivity.

Start by giving your child a book or magazine article about the sport you're considering, and let him develop an interest gradually. Even very young children can benefit from this approach if you scale it down to their level with picture books or photos cut out of magazines. Then, if you haven't already done so, let your child look at the brochures you've collected about the upcoming adventure. If you're going to a resort area, point out that there are a variety of activities for children, in addition to the primary activity of horseback riding, or skiing or whatever. If your child is still reluctant, let him know that his or her participation is not required. If your child is terrified of horses, for instance, he or she can spend time on a dude ranch learning camp crafts or swimming in the lake.

To introduce kids to a new spectator sport, the logical place to start is at home in front of the television set. But forget logic—kids who are lukewarm to ice hockey on TV will probably think it's totally cool if you take them to a real live game in a big arena. There's nothing like the action of a real game, with the fans cheering all around you and the junk food flowing through the crowds, to spark a little interest in a previously apathetic kid.

Most important of all, remember that kids hate to be pressured, and are smart enough to resent it when they think a parent is sending the message, "Like this sport or I won't like *you*." Try to convey to your children that there are some terrific sports experiences out there, that you hope they'll share your enthusiasm for the sport you've chosen but that you respect their right to feel otherwise.

And lastly, don't oversell the trip to your kids ahead of time. Sure, a little advance P.R. is a good idea, but many a fine vacation has been ruined by the fact that everyone's expectations were so high that no reality could possibly live up to it.

If you can do all that, congratulations! You'll undoubtedly have a successful adventure with your kids.

WHAT TO TAKE AND HOW TO PACK IT

I have one rule about packing for travel: No matter where you're going or what time of year, always take a bathing suit and a sweater. This may sound like an oversimplification, but if you look a little deeper you'll realize that

there's a travel philosophy at work here, not just a trip tip. The idea is that you should always be prepared for the unexpected, both in terms of what you've brought along and in your mental attitude as well. So what if you're only going on an overnight business trip to Chicago in the middle of January? There might be an indoor swimming pool at your hotel—just the thing to relax you after a tense meeting. So what if your adventure vacation is Death Valley in July? It can be very cold in the desert after the sun goes down.

Extend this "expect the unexpected" philosophy a little bit, and you'll get the general idea about packing for family adventure vacations. It means that you'll probably want to take a first-aid kit, especially if you're going whitewater rafting; you'll want to take rain gear if you're going sailing; and you'll want to take a little extra cash, even on a wilderness trip where there's no place to spend it. And of course you'll take a bathing suit and a sweater no matter what!

When packing for young children, the best rule of thumb is: Take along twice as much clothing for each child per day as for adults. Kids get dirty and need to change more often during the course of a day. And teenagers often *choose* to change their clothes frequently. So, unless you know there will be a laundromat available at your vacation destination, don't skimp on packing casual clothes for the kids. On the other hand, don't pack a lot of dress-up clothes for your adventure vacation, because in most cases you and your children will never wear them.

Do take warm pajamas for your children, especially if you will be sleeping in air-conditioned rooms. Also, if possible, pack an extra pair of shoes for each child. If one pair of sneakers gets soaked, you'll be grateful you have a spare pair on hand.

Beyond the issue of how much clothing to pack, children have their own specific needs when it comes to travel. Generally speaking, the advice you hear a lot—take along toys, books, and other materials to keep your kids happy and occupied—is good up to a point. My experience has been that the bags full of toys and games that were packed into the trunk, or loaded into a carry-on bag for the plane, or stuffed into the back seat of the car, were used only during the first two to three hours of the trip. After that, the excitement of actually being on vacation, of going in search of some new adventure, began to take hold. So there's no need to overdo it.

On the other hand, respect your child's need to feel he can take a part of his safe and familiar home environment with him. Just knowing that a well-loved toy is there can help reduce anxiety for a very young child. Even older children like to think that there are some aspects of the trip they can control. A case in point: When I was 14 years old, my family took a trip to the World's Fair in New York.

Although almost every aspect of the trip had been planned without my input, my parents left it entirely to me to decide which clothes and how many I would bring. My decision, as it turned out, was to bring every single article of clothing I owned—so many garments that they filled the largest piece of luggage in my parents' set, an enormous suitcase so oversized it had never been used before! Of course I didn't need or use all those clothes on our vacation, but I never forgot the generosity my parents had shown in letting me bring along a "security" wardrobe. That privilege was one of the things that made the trip memorable, even before it began.

But let's get real! You can't let your teenagers take along trunks full of clothes on a whitewater rafting trip. And for that matter, a bag full of toys isn't too practical in the wilderness, either. So use common sense and try to help your child weigh the importance of each item he or she wants to bring. Here are some guidelines for each age group, to help you sort out what will be useful from what will be superfluous.

▶ For kids of any age, a portable tape recorder and a variety of tapes is a great travel/entertainment item. In the car, the whole family can enjoy the music or comedy, and books on tape really make the time fly. Don't forget to bring headphones for the tape recorder, especially when your children's taste in music gets a little too wild for you!

▶ Some families have a rule with kids beginning at age seven or eight: They may bring anything they can carry themselves. The problem with that rule is that your kids will swear they can carry what they've packed until they're halfway down the airport concourse. Then the whining begins. To prevent such miscalculations, have your kids pack their bags a few days early and carry them around during a family errand, as a trial run. Inevitably they'll rethink and repack, eliminating something.

▶ Instead of bringing a whole bag of toys your kids may be tired of, try buying one new small toy for each child. Hand them out just after you leave the house. It doesn't have to be something big or expensive, but one new toy will hold your child's attention longer than several old ones.

▶ For babies and toddlers, don't forget to bring a thermometer, petroleum jelly and acetaminophen. Also, take your stroller no matter what. Even if it seems inappropriate for your main activity, it will come in handy in a variety of places. You'll use it to tote your baby around from one building to another on a dude ranch, or in the airport. And you might even use it as a place to park your baby safely around a campfire.

▶ Be sure to bring a stuffed animal or special blanket for a younger child. The comforts of home, away from home, somehow become a priority at bedtime.

▶ Bring digging toys. They are great on any kind of outdoor sports adventure.

▶ For car travel, some form of highway bingo is a must. Look for the flat cardboard version with sliding plastic windows instead of loose pieces. It takes up less room than other travel bingo games. This version, made by Regal Games Manufacturing Company, is sometimes sold in bookstores.

▶ Take your own soap, especially if you or your children have sensitive skin.

▶ Cards, puzzles and activity books, especially the ones with invisible ink and magic pens (often sold at airports) are great time fillers for airplane trips and beyond.

▶ If your adventure takes you to a family camp or group outing with many families and children involved, make nametags for small children to wear around their necks. Pack them in your daily tote bag, so you'll have them handy.

▶ If your child has his or her own camera, bring it as well as your own. Kids often enjoy taking their own snapshots as mementos of the trip; they *don't* enjoy lending their cameras to their parents every two minutes. It spoils the fun of having a camera of one's own.

Once you've decided what to take on your trip, your next goal is to get it sensibly packed. There are two very different strategies to choose from. One is to pack each person's clothing and gear in a separate bag. This works really well if you're traveling by air to a destination and then staying put, or on any trip in which your luggage will be carried for you. The premise is that, although you are taking along a number of bags, it's easier for each person to dig through his or her own suitcase looking for a favorite t-shirt, rather than for one person (usually a parent) to be responsible for finding any given item in one huge trunk. Even if your children are too young to get their own things, it's easier for you to find them if they are separate from your belongings.

The other strategy, however, is to pack a number of small bags. One bag contains pajamas and toiletries for the entire family. Each of the other small bags contains clothing for the whole family for one or two days. Packing this way can be an organizational challenge, to be sure. But this strategy works well when you're traveling long distances by car. You only need to carry two small bags into the motel room each night: the pajama bag and one day's worth of clothes. All the other luggage stays in the car.

In any case, it's always smart to pack the pajamas and toiletries on top, or in a separate bag, so you can get to them easily when you arrive at your lodgings on that first night.

The most important packing tip of all: Pack everything a full day in advance of your departure. There's no better way to spoil a good vacation than to start out with a lot of last minute rushing around. Packing, even when you travel light, is a time-consuming chore, so leave plenty of time and don't worry about the clothes getting twice as wrinkled. That's what travel irons are for.

AIR TRAVEL WITH KIDS

It takes many years of traveling with children to figure out all the tricks that make air travel simple. By the time parents who travel infrequently have figured out the tricks, their children have grown up. All the tips and tricks I've amassed over the years from friends, family, and my own airplane experiences are here for you to pick and choose the ones that match your needs.

▶ Remember to get your seat assignments in advance. Ask for the bulkhead seats if you'll be traveling with a baby or a very active toddler. Choose a combination of aisle and window seats for most other family configurations. Remember that bulkhead seats don't have folding tray tables, which may figure in your in-flight activities. And the armrests in the bulkhead seats don't lift up, making it harder for children to nap. If two or more of your children are teenagers or pre-teens, you may want to let them sit by themselves, a few seats behind you, for instance. They'll appreciate the freedom, and so will you.

▶ Order your child's meals well in advance. Most airlines have several different categories of meals available, including children's meals, as well as adult vegetarian meals and sometimes a salad plate. The child's meal is usually a hamburger or hot dog, so ask the airline for specifics and choose accordingly. The salad plate can be a child's delight: fruit and cottage cheese or yogurt. Most airlines require at least 24 hours notice, though, so plan ahead.

▶ Even though you have ordered your children's meals well in advance, bring your own snacks along on the plane. Food and drink are never served until the flight is well underway—that is, until you and your family are starved. Boxes of juice, raisins, pieces of fruit or crackers are virtual necessities for airplane travel.

▶ Be sure to bring gum or hard candies for your children to suck on during take-off and landing, when the changes in air pressure often cause ear discomfort. And if your child has allergies or a cold, ask your pediatrician about using an antihistamine about 30 minutes before take-off or landing. If your child has a cold, ask about a decongestant/antihistimine combination. It can help alleviate the congestion which causes ear problems for so many infants and children.

▶ What about a truly active child—or any toddler? My philosophy is to put them in an aisle seat and let them explore the airplane, whenever it's safe and convenient for other passengers, under the supervision of a parent or older sibling. Of course, it's not a good idea to let your toddler run around while the flight attendants are serving meals. But in the confined and stuffy atmosphere of an airplane, most people agree that smiling, happy, curious children are like a breath of fresh air. Crying children, on the other hand, are not so readily tolerated, which is why you should go ahead and let your toddler romp. Keeping them as happy as possible is best for everyone.

▶ Flights longer than three hours usually have movies, while shorter flights do not. Whether your children want to see the movie or not, you may want to request headphones for the whole family. There are music and comedy channels to listen to, and turning the dial will keep your children busy for a while. If you advise the flight attendant that your kids aren't going to view the movie, you probably won't have to pay the headphone charge.

ACCOMMODATIONS

When traveling with children there are a variety of places to stay, apart from the most obvious motel at the off-ramp of a major highway. Depending on the kind of sports adventure you're planning, you may want to stay at a campground, a cabin in a state park, a hotel, a resort area, or even a bed-and-breakfast. The latter are sometimes less well-known and often less well-advertised, but can provide a fine, reasonably priced alternative to the standard motel chains. To find out about bed-and-breakfasts, as well as other unique accommodations at or en route to your vacation destination, contact the appropriate Chamber of Commerce or state Department of Tourism.

For a family of four or more, especially with older children, it's much easier to manage during your vacation if you can afford accommodations in a larger space—a cabin, hotel suite or two adjoining rooms, for instance. Children from the age of about 10 and up can occupy an adjoining hotel or motel room without constant supervision. In fact, your teenaged sons or daughters may require the privacy that two rooms can provide. It's also great for parents to be able to read or watch television while the children are sleeping peacefully in the adjoining room—or the teenagers are gooning out on late-night horror movies. If you're considering adjoining hotel rooms, investigate the all-suites hotels, as they often offer a better value with extras such as continental breakfast included in the suite rate.

In any case, be sure to establish some ground rules regarding the use of room service, not opening the door to strangers, and so forth. Also remember to read and discuss with your children the fire escape route. By law it must be posted on the inside of the room door in all hotels.

LIVING IN ONE ROOM

Not all families can afford the luxury of a suite or adjoining hotel rooms. And if your children are quite young, you may not require the extra space. Living in one room, though, is a bit of a balancing act, requiring some special coping techniques. For instance, how do you get your kids to bed at a decent hour, without being forced to go to sleep then yourself? Do you have to sit in the dark from 8:30 on?

This is an easy one, sort of. If your kids are used to sleeping in absolute pitch darkness, you tuck them in, turn out the lights, and hide in the bathroom with a good book for about 30 minutes or so. Take the pillows from your bed and stretch out in the tub, if necessary! When your kids have gone to sleep, you can sneak back into the room and turn on a light. (If your kids can go to sleep with you in the room, you may want to invest in a mini-reading lamp that clips on to your book—it sure beats doing bathroom duty!) You can even watch TV if you keep the sound low at first, increasing it only gradually.

If your kids prefer to have a night light on, carefully drape a towel over the lampshade of one of the bedside lamps. Be careful to leave the space above the lightbulb open, so the towel doesn't get too hot, and keep an eye on it. (Needless to say, you don't want to start a hotel fire!) Then go into the bathroom as above, and wait for the kiddies to conk out. When you go to sleep, you can turn out the towel "night light," and leave the bathroom light on for the kids.

Another tip for motel/hotel room living is to use your ice bucket as a mini-refrigerator if the room isn't equipped with one. Ice is almost always free, so you can refill the bucket as often as you like. If necessary, you might request that housekeeping bring you a second ice bucket so you can keep twice as many containers of milk, juice and yogurt cool. Overnight, wrap the packed bucket in a towel for added insulation. The ice may have melted by morning, but you'll still have cold juice and milk for the cereal you bought at a market the night before. Of course, if you're traveling by car, you may have your own cooler with you, in which case you can simply use that. Check ahead to make sure that the motel/hotel at which you are staying doesn't have regulations prohibiting food in the rooms—some places enforce this regulation.

Finally, don't be afraid to move the furniture around if it doesn't suit your needs. Perhaps there's a lamp too far from the bed for reading. Or a table that's simply in the way. Feel free to rearrange anything that isn't bolted down, or even ask the management to remove a few chairs, for instance, if it would give your family more breathing room.

FANTASTIC TRIPS FOR THE SPORTS SPECTATOR

Picture this: You fly to Dodgertown, the Dodgers' spring training complex in Vero Beach, Florida, check into your room, take a shower, loosen up a little, put on a team uniform and then head for the baseball diamond to take a little batting practice with former Dodgers greats. You're playing ball with the major leaguers! And not for just one day—this goes on for a whole week! You may even win camp Rookie of the Year. And it will only cost you about $4000! It's the all-time best, most self-indulgent professional sports fan's fantasy ever.

Well, it's a fantasy come true, all right. But it's not a fantasy trip you'll be taking with the whole family, because mock spring training camp sessions at Dodgertown are not open to children, for any price.

There are, however, half a dozen fabulous trips that you *can* take with your family of sports fans—some of which give you the chance to see your favorite athletes up close and off the playing field, and all of which give you the opportunity to extend your enjoyment of the sport. Depending on your family's interests, you might choose a trip to a pro football team's summer training camp, or a trip to the annual NBA draft. And why confine baseball to a mere seven months when you can visit the Baseball Hall of Fame during Christmas vacation, or make an appearance at spring training in March? And for sheer hype and excitement, there's nothing like the Super Bowl—a glamorous adventure no matter who's playing.

These are adventure trips for die-hard fans of the four most popular professional team sports in America: baseball, football, basketball and hockey. Baseball comes first because, with more than 45 million fans attending major league games in an average year, it is the single most popular professional team sport in the country. Visiting the Baseball Hall of Fame may not be a "Field of Dreams," but it's the next best thing. Have fun!

BASEBALL

SPRING TRAINING

How would you like to sit in a small, intimate baseball park on a perfectly clear sunny day and watch all of your favorite big league baseball players talking, laughing, warming up and working out together? A few hours later, another major league team will show up for a game, and the mood will be decidedly friendly. Rival players joke with each other, coaches exchange friendly hellos or share anecdotes. After the game, you can join the players as they walk casually along a path toward the clubhouse several hundred feet away from and outside of the ball field.

That's the scene at baseball's spring training, held every year for six weeks from mid-February to the end of March in Florida and Arizona. For a baseball-loving family, there's no better family adventure than a trip to spring training, which is always open to the public and offers countless opportunities to see superstar baseball players in settings that are more informal and intimate than what the average fan encounters at home. There's a magical atmosphere at spring training—it's an almost sweetly innocent time. Most of the players are relaxed and optimistic about the season ahead, the weather is good, and baseball is played as if it's still a *game*, in the best, least commercial sense of the word.

Spring training is a fan's big chance to hang out around the players and talk to them, get their autographs, or take their photographs. Sometimes they'll even pose with you or your kids after one of the many exhibition games that are played. It's also a chance to see National League clubs playing against American League clubs. And it's a chance to see baseball superstars of the past, some of them Hall of Famers, who serve as coaches or instructors, or simply hang out at one club or another. The fact that so many of them come back long after they have retired should tell you something about the joys of spring training.

Of course there's another side to spring training that is actually serious business. Managers and coaches are looking at rookie players, deciding whether or not they've got what it takes to play in the majors, and simultaneously evaluating veteran players who are often hustling to keep their jobs or to make a comeback. As an observer at spring training, you can nearly read the story on the players' faces: A happy, relaxed, joking demeanor belongs to the secure player whose career is not in jeopardy. The focused, hard-working, isolated and tense player is usually struggling for a break or a comeback from an injury or a bad year.

Of the 26 major league teams, eight hold their spring training in Arizona. The rest are headquartered in three clusters in Florida. The Central Florida cluster of five towns with teams are Plant City, Lakeland, Winter Haven, Haines City and Kissimmee. On the Gulf Coast there are seven training camps that run in a string about 125 miles long, straight down the western coast of Florida. From north to south, the Gulf Coast cluster includes Dunedin, Clearwater, St. Petersburg, Bradenton, Sarasota, Port Charlotte and Fort Myers. The third cluster in Florida includes six teams that train

in cities on the Atlantic Coast, including Vero Beach, Port St. Lucie, West Palm Beach, Fort Lauderdale and Miami.

If you are particularly ambitious and want to visit a lot of training camps, you can plan a tour of the Central Florida training camps along with some of the Gulf Coast cities. Those training sites would include Plant City, Lakeland, Kissimmee, Haines City, Winter Haven, Dunedin, Clearwater, Bradenton and St. Petersburg—all within 100 miles of each other. Check a map to get an idea of distances and locations.

Spring training begins earlier in Arizona, with most teams reporting in mid-February. Most of the Arizona training camps are clustered around Phoenix, so it's very easy for fans to visit several camps, even on a short trip. Most of the west coast teams train in Arizona because it's closer for them than Florida, but, by tradition, the Chicago Cubs, Cleveland Indians and Milwaukee Brewers camps are also in Arizona, even though Florida would be closer. (And the Los Angeles Dodgers' camp is in Florida.)

A complete list of teams and training sites is given below, accurate as of 1990. Training sites can change, however, so you should check with a particular team's home office before you make your plans.

Teams training in Florida:

Atlanta Braves—West Palm Beach
Cincinnati Reds—Plant City
Houston Astros—Kissimmee
Los Angeles Dodgers—Vero Beach
Montreal Expos—West Palm Beach
New York Mets—Port St. Lucie
Philadelphia Phillies—Clearwater
Pittsburgh Pirates—Bradenton
St. Louis Cardinals—St. Petersburg
Baltimore Orioles—Early spring training in Sarasota, then they move
    to Miami
Boston Red Sox—Winter Haven
Chicago White Sox—Sarasota
Detroit Tigers—Lakeland
Kansas City Royals—Haines City
Minnesota Twins—Fort Myers
New York Yankees—Ft. Lauderdale
Texas Rangers—Port Charlotte
Toronto Blue Jays—Dunedin

Teams training in Arizona:

> California Angels—Early spring training in Mesa, then they move to
>   Palm Springs, California
> Chicago Cubs—Mesa
> Cleveland Indians—Tucson
> Milwaukee Brewers—Chandler
> Oakland Athletics—Phoenix
> San Diego Padres—Yuma
> San Francisco Giants—Scottsdale
> Seattle Mariners—Tempe

With the training sites in such close geographical proximity, it's possible for a family to visit several different spring training camps in a week-long vacation. And if some family members are less than gung-ho about spring training, there's always the temptation of a side trip to Disney World, Epcot or Disney/ MGM Studios, located very near the central Florida training camps. In Arizona, there are a number of golf and tennis resorts which offer a variety of activities for the whole family. Check with your travel agent for more details.

When to Go

In Florida, the early weeks of spring training, from mid-February to the beginning of March, are a prime time to see pitchers and catchers working out together, as these players report early so they will be ready when the rest of the team arrives. In early March, the entire team begins to work out together—running, doing weight training, taking batting and fielding practice and playing intrasquad games. By the middle of March, the primary focus is on playing exhibition games against other major league teams. Tickets to these games are sold through ticket offices at the stadiums where the games are played. Tickets are often available on short notice, but many games do sell out so you might want to purchase tickets early. Contact your favorite team's home office in early January and ask for information about spring training exhibition games.

Whether you're headed for Florida or Arizona, check with the specific ball clubs for exact reporting dates in the year you plan to make your pilgrimage. In 1990, a labor dispute delayed the opening of the camps and ruined many vacations.

For more information about spring training, you might want to read *Cactus League Road Trip* and *Grapefruit League Road Trip* (Stephen Greene Press), two books about—you guessed it—spring training in Arizona and Florida respectively. Authors Ken Coleman and Dan Valenti offer colorful descriptions of the teams and fields in each location and tips about where to stay while you're there.

NATIONAL BASEBALL HALL OF FAME AND MUSEUM
Cooperstown, New York

Cooperstown, New York, named for James Fenimore Cooper and nestled beside the shimmering Otsego Lake which Cooper called "Glimmerglass," is a jewel of a small town with the self-contained serenity that small towns everywhere used to exhibit. Park benches dot the landscape near the lake, white steeples rise above the red brick buildings of commerce, trees line the streets and overhang the walkways connecting one point of interest to another. And everywhere you look there are flower boxes and flags. At the heart of it all is Cooperstown's most famous museum, the National Baseball Hall of Fame.

The Hall of Fame itself occupies a graceful brick building of traditional American architectural style—the kind of building that might have been a school or a town hall fifty years ago. Inside it's a well-designed contemporary museum with first-rate displays, engaging media presentations, and interactive computer exhibits, all carefully blended to evoke both nostalgia for baseball's past and enthusiasm for baseball's future.

In four floors of exhibits, you'll see not just a little bit of everything but a lot of everything. Players' mementos are the cornerstone of the museum: Babe Ruth's bat, ball and uniform from his 60th home run are on display, as are Willie Mays's shoes, Casey Stengel's scorebook, Ted Williams's sunglasses and some umpiring equipment used by Tom Connolly in the early 1900s. Even the original hundred-year-old Doubleday baseball is on view. Scuffed, dirty and yellowing with age, these balls, bats, masks and shoes are almost shrines unto themselves, so beautifully are they displayed. But the memorabilia is just the beginning. There are specialty exhibits such as the present-day locker room display with each team's uniforms. There's an IBM interactive touch-screen computer which allows visitors to search for statistics and career information about each Hall of Famer. There's a tribute to Women in Baseball, chronicling the women's professional leagues of the 1940s and '50s. And there's a special exhibit devoted to the early Negro Leagues.

In fact, the range and depth of the Hall of Fame exhibits is so extensive that many visitors spend more than one day here. And why not? The museum has so much visual appeal that children often don't want to leave. The 200-seat theater, for instance, is a display in itself, designed to look like a baseball stadium with flags and banners and a Coca-Cola scoreboard.

In another location, the classic Abbott and Costello comedy routine, "Who's on First?" is shown on a video monitor. And, of course, there is the Hall of Fame Gallery itself, a majestic space wherein more than 200 baseball greats are immortalized, with a bronze plaque for each player.

In late July or early August of each year, the new Hall of Fame inductees are officially welcomed to the museum in an induction ceremony which is free and open to the public. Many older Hall of Famers are often present as well, making this a great chance to see baseball legends in person and share the magic of a baseball tradition—if you don't mind crowds. The day after the induction ceremonies, the annual major league Hall of Fame game is played at Doubleday Field, just one block from the museum. The game features an American League team against a National League team, with the teams selected each year after both leagues have prepared their season's schedule. Tickets for the Hall of Fame game are available on a first-come, first-served basis from Ticketron beginning in March of each year.

One important note: If you're traveling some distance to attend the induction ceremonies, you'll need to plan well in advance, since hotels and motels in Cooperstown are reserved a full year ahead of time. Cooperstown has a number of exceptional accommodations, including a wonderful old resort hotel named the Otesaga, and the Cooper Motor Inn, a restored Victorian mansion. For more information, contact the Cooperstown Chamber of Commerce at (607) 547-9983.

And finally, remember that during the induction week, the small town will be bulging at the seams with crowds, which means that you might have to stand in line for a hamburger—or fight a mighty mob of people for a glimpse of the baseball greats!

Affiliated with the Hall of Fame, but in its own separate building, is the National Baseball Library, an extensive facility containing not only books and periodicals but also many photo exhibits and television monitor displays with videotapes of various teams. The library is open to the public seven days a week in summer, Monday through Friday the rest of the year.

Cooperstown has a lot to offer the vacationing family, with water sports available on Lake Otsego and two other noteworthy tourist attractions in town: The Farmer's Museum recreates rural 18th century life in upstate New York, while the Fenimore House is home to the New York State Historical Association. Several fine old hotels offer accommodations and use of recreational facilities, including the Leatherstocking Golf Course.

The National Baseball Hall of Fame is open every day of the year except Christmas, Thanksgiving and New Year's Day. Admission is $6 for adults, $2.50 for children ages 7–15. Combination tickets for admission to all three of Cooperstown's museums are also available.

For more information contact National Baseball Hall of Fame, P.O. Box 590, Cooperstown, NY 13326. Phone (607) 547-9988.

FOOTBALL

PRO FOOTBALL HALL OF FAME
Canton, Ohio

The first question most people ask about the Pro Football Hall of Fame is, "Why is it in Canton, Ohio?" What they mean is, why is the Hall of Fame located in a city with no national sports affiliation, and what does Canton have to do with football anyway?

The fact is that Canton, Ohio, is nothing if not wildly enthusiastic about football—always has been, always will be. And there's plenty of football history there: The American Professional Football Association, forerunner of the NFL, was founded in Canton in 1920, and early football legend Jim Thorpe played his first pro football with the Canton Bulldogs in 1915. So it was no surprise when Canton citizens launched a well-organized campaign to have their city designated as the official Hall of Fame site. Approval was given in 1961, the first building was completed in 1963, and the museum has been growing ever since.

Today, this museum is a dream come true for football fans, a trip down memory lane with the chance to revisit favorite football seasons, players and games. The 51,000-square-foot modern facility contains a vast array of exhibits, many of them interactive. On the main floor, in the rotunda, you'll find a chronological history of football from 1892 to the present, including special exhibits highlighting the careers of Johnny Unitas, Jim Thorpe and Walter Payton, the oldest football in the Hall's collection, and a video presentation of 16 Fantastic Finishes. Then you'll come to the Enshrinement Galleries where each Hall of Famer is honored. Video presentations are featured here as well, including a program called "The Legends of the Game" which contains interviews with enshrinees. The Super Bowl Room contains mementos, photos, trophies, newspaper accounts and a video summary of all the Super Bowls played. And the exhibits go on and on. There's a fan enthusiasm display, a room full of players' mementos (Joe Namath's jersey, O.J. Simpson's helmet, the ice tongs used by Red Grange while working his way through college as an iceman), a display chronicling the Black Man in Pro Football, an exhibit of

team uniforms, a trophy display, quiz machines, recorded radio broadcasts—enough, in other words, to keep you and your kids busy a full day or more. As if this isn't enough, the ground floor of the museum has a movie theater where a different short film is shown each hour on the hour at no additional charge. Among the films available: "Football Funnies" and "Great Super Bowl Moments." You can even request a specific film and they'll try to work it into the schedule. If you stay all day, you could see eight different films!

The most exciting time to go, of course, is for the annual induction ceremony for newly elected Hall of Famers. It's held every year during the last week of July or first week of August, and it's free and open to the public. The ceremony itself takes place outdoors on the steps of the Hall of Fame, usually on a Saturday morning. The new inductees are there, so bring your camera and supply each kid with a pen and paper for autograph-seeking. In the afternoon, following the enshrinement, you can attend the AFC-NFC Hall of Fame Football Game if you've ordered tickets ahead of time. The game is held in a high school stadium directly across the street from the museum. With so much to do on enshrinement day, you'll want to make your trip a two-day visit so you'll have plenty of time to see the Hall of Fame itself as well. The museum calls this Football's Greatest Weekend, and it might be just the ticket for you and your family, too!

The Pro Football Hall of Fame is open every day of the year except Christmas. Daily hours are from 9 a.m. to 8 p.m. in summer, and from 9 a.m. to 5 p.m. the rest of the year. Admission is $4.00 for adults; $1.50 for children ages 5 to 13; or $10 for the whole family.

To obtain tickets for the annual AFC-NFC Hall of Fame Game, call or write the Hall of Fame in December or January preceding the game you want to attend, and ask to be placed on the mailing list. You'll be sent an application for tickets; return it promptly! Tickets are sold on a first-come, first-served basis, and the games always sell out. The schedule for the next eight years is:

> 1991—Miami Dolphins vs. Detroit Lions
> 1992—New York Jets vs. Philadelphia Eagles
> 1993—Los Angeles Raiders vs. Green Bay Packers
> 1994—Denver Broncos vs. Dallas Cowboys
> 1995—San Diego Chargers vs. Atlanta Falcons
> 1996—Indianapolis Colts vs. New Orleans Saints
> 1997—Seattle Seahawks vs. Minnesota Vikings
> 1998—Pittsburgh Steelers vs. Tampa Bay Buccaneers

For more information contact the Pro Football Hall of Fame, 2121 George Halas Drive NW, Canton, Ohio 44708. Phone (216) 456-8207.

PRO FOOTBALL SUMMER TRAINING CAMPS

Every summer about mid-July, the professional football teams begin to assemble in various training camps to get in shape for the fall season. In many cases, these training sessions are open to the public, free of charge. It's not quite like going to baseball's spring training camps, because the teams don't play each other and the camps are usually held close to home turf. But you'll get to see your favorite superstars grunting and groaning, sweating and moaning, as they work out and run through drills and practice offense against defense in the blistering sun. For some of us, it's agony just to watch football in warm weather—but the agony can be worthwhile. You might get the chance to grab an autograph, take some snapshots or catch a player's smile as he heads for the locker room at the end of the day. And in any case, you'll get a different view of the sport from that seen on network television. Up close, the players look more human, their blows look more powerful, their efforts look more strenuous. It's all very *real*.

Summer training for most teams runs from mid-July to mid-August, but check with the teams for specific dates and locations. Some teams train at a nearby college, using the school's playing field by day and housing the players in dormitories at night. For instance, the Miami Dolphins train at St. Thomas University in Miami, the Los Angeles Rams train at the University of California at Irvine and the San Francisco 49ers use Sierra Community College in Rockland, California. Other teams have their own training facilities, separate from the stadium. And some teams—notably the New Orleans Saints—travel quite some distance from "home." The Saints train at the University of Wisconsin in Lacrosse, Wisconsin, because the heat and humidity in New Orleans are almost unbearable in July.

For more information, write or call the teams directly. A complete listing of NFL team addresses can be found in the Appendix beginning on page 133.

THE SUPER BOWL

How do you get tickets to the Super Bowl? Are they outrageously expensive? Does it cost a fortune to eat and sleep in Super Bowl territory? And is it really worth going? Those are good questions, worthy of good answers.

Question #1: There are basically two ways to get tickets to the Super Bowl. If you are a season ticket holder for any NFL team, your team will give you the opportunity to enter a lottery. Those fans selected at random in the team lotteries may buy tickets. The second way is to write to the NFL between February 1 and June 1. The NFL has a certain number of seats available, and holds its own lottery for the people who have requested Super Bowl tickets from the NFL by mail. But your chances of being selected are only about 1 in 40—and even if you are selected in the NFL lottery, you will only be able to buy two tickets. So what does a family of four do? Ask *all* your friends to enter the NFL lottery, too—and cross your fingers!

Question #2: Super Bowl tickets cost around $125 each in recent years (and are rising), which is about $100 more than individual game tickets during the season. You can also find tickets available from brokers for much higher prices. Check your local newspaper classifieds if you're a glutton for this particular kind of punishment.

Question #3: Most hotels and restaurants in the Super Bowl city raise their rates for this period, or at the very least they offer no discounts. And reservations must be made well in advance. If you win the lottery and plan to go, talk with a travel agent or the local Chamber of Commerce about some alternative housing arrangements. Bed-and-breakfasts, for example, may be cheaper and more readily available. On the other hand, part of the fun of going to the Super Bowl is getting caught up in all the excitement, catching the Super Bowl fever. And since you'll only be there for a weekend, you may find that it's worth it to splurge on hotel accommodations right in the heart of all the goings-on.

Question #4: Is is worth going to? That depends on your level of fanaticism about football and your ability to afford the outing. But it's probably safe to say that if you and your kids like football, you'll love the aura that accompanies a trip to the sport's big finale. And let's face it: The kids will *cherish* the opportunity to tell their friends about being on the scene in person. Even if the game itself falls flat, the memories will almost certainly take on a grand glow.

For more information contact the National Football League at 410 Park Avenue, New York, N.Y. 10022. Phone (212) 758-1500.

BASKETBALL

Professional basketball is fast-paced and jam-packed with excitement, so it's not surprising to learn that the annual NBA draft is just the same. The draft, which is the pre-season selection of new players, is held in New York City each year during the last week of June. It consists of the first two rounds only, with each team being given five minutes to make their first-round picks, and only two or three minutes in the second round. The top 15 or 20 players being drafted are usually there in person, and you could be, too! The draft, which is usually held in a large public arena or convention center, is free and open to the public with seating on a first-come, first-served basis. The whole proceeding takes about three hours and is broadcast live on network television, with highlights projected on big-screen monitors throughout the convention center. But if you're on the spot you'll see it *all*—not just the highlights selected by the media. You'll see the expressions on the players' faces, and can see how they feel at the moment their futures and fates are being decided.

There could also be autograph opportunities at the NBA draft—and what sports-minded kid doesn't love autographs? In fact, your kids could be among the first people to request autographs from the newly-drafted players. Just think how much fun your family will have watching basketball in the months and years ahead, as those young players make their way through their rookie years and continue to grow professionally. And all the while your family will remember they were there on the day these players were drafted by the NBA.

If you've always wanted to see New York City, this is a great excuse to do it—and fortunately the draft takes place during the summer, when the kids are out of school. Needless to say, a vacation in New York City is a big undertaking, and you will probably be happiest if you get a travel agent to help you plan the trip.

For more information about the NBA draft, including specific times and dates, contact the National Basketball Association, 645 Fifth Avenue, New York, N.Y. 10022. Phone (212) 826-7000.

BASKETBALL HALL OF FAME
Springfield, Massachussetts

In recent years, the key words in museum exhibits have been "interactive" and "hands-on." Give the museum-goer something to do, and chances are he or she is more likely to have a memorable experience. Well, that approach has been executed with tremendous success at the Basketball Hall of Fame, where, for instance, visitors are offered the opportunity to shoot baskets to their hearts' content on an ingenious device called the "Spalding Sidewalk." This moving sidewalk carries you past ten baskets of different heights. As soon as you take a shot, you get another ball and take your next shot. It's a kid's dream come true, though you'll probably see more than a couple of grown-ups taking a turn or two as well.

Another popular feature at the Hall of Fame is the exhibit called "How High is Up?" where you will test your vertical leaping ability by jumping up to hit a series of paddles. And for the strictly cerebral fan, there's an interactive video called the "Hall of Fame Challenge," in which visitors test their knowledge of basketball against a computer.

There are the usual assortment of video presentations, historical exhibits, a gift shop and, of course, the actual Hall of Fame for the enshrinees. All together, more than 170 individuals and four teams are honored in the Basketball Hall of Fame. The facility is impressive, with 40,000 square feet on three levels— enough space to include not only professional basketball but also college ball, women's basketball, and the international professional teams.

The annual induction ceremony is a terrific event, held the second weekend in May, at which time the Hall of Fame sponsors a free three-hour basketball lecture and demonstration for boys and girls. It's conducted by past Hall of Famers, and as many as 12,000 kids can attend. Also on the slate that weekend is an awards banquet, which is open to the public. Up to 17,000 people can be accommodated.

The Basketball Hall of Fame is open from 9 a.m. to 5 p.m., every day of the year except Thanksgiving, Christmas and New Year's Day. Admission is $5 for adults, $3 for students ages 9–15, free for children under 8.

For more information, contact the Basketball Hall of Fame, P.O. Box 179, Springfield, Mass. 01101-0179. Phone (413) 781-6500.

HOCKEY

With one-third of the National Hockey League teams located in Canada, and most of the others clustered in the North and Northeast, professional hockey is a fairly regional sport. For many families, just taking a trip to see an NHL game would be an adventure in itself. Hard-core fans, on the other hand, want something more; they want to eat, sleep and dream hockey.

If you happen to live near the right team, you can do just that, because several of the teams have an "open practice session" policy which allows fans to hang out around the ice rink during any and all practices. For instance, the New York Islanders practice at Cantiague Park in Hicksville, New York, and all practices are open to the public. The ice rink charges a small fee of $2 per person to Nassau County residents who show a Leisure Pass. (A Leisure Pass costs $5 per year and admits county residents to all Nassau County parks.) Nonresidents pay $6 per person to watch the Islanders practice.

Other teams make selected practice sessions open to the public, some-times using the event as a fund-raiser for charity. One particularly success-ful event is the annual food drive sponsored by the Detroit Red Wings in which the fans are invited to attend a practice session at Joe Louis Arena in downtown Detroit, and the price of admission is two cans of food per person. As many as 8,000 people have turned up for this event in one year, and in 1989, the Red Wings collected more than 15 tons of food. This is the perfect kind of event for a family sports adventure because it offers your kids the excitement of being in an ice arena with thousands of other enthu-siastic fans, plus the chance to do something beneficial to the community—and the cost to you is minimal. Certain regular Red Wings practice sessions, which are held at Oak Park Arena (in the suburb of the same name), are also open to the public.

The Buffalo Sabres have a similar once-a-year public practice session, held in Memorial Auditorium during the week after Christmas. This event is usually attended by about 15,000 screaming kids, and it's more of a show than a real practice. The price of admission is one Kodak film box-top—the session is co-sponsored by Kodak—and each fan gets to take home a poster at the end of the day. You can also watch the Sabres training at Sabreland in Wheatfield, New York.

To give your family sports adventure an international flavor, you might want to visit one of the Canadian teams. Besides the obvious hockey appeal, your kids will love the Canadian money and will feel very sophisticated hav-ing traveled to a country in which many public signs and instructions appear in both English and French.

In any case, call or write the teams for information, as practice session policies vary from team to team, and may have changed since this writing. A complete listing of the NHL teams with addresses and phone numbers can be found in the Appendix on page 133.

HOCKEY HALLS OF FAME

Though not as grand as their counterparts in baseball or basketball, the U.S. Hockey Hall of Fame in Eveleth, Minnesota, and the Hockey Hall of Fame in Toronto, Ontario, should be kept in mind by hockey lovers. The U.S. Hall of Fame, for instance, has a theater, a grand hall for the enshrinees and a gift shop—no interactive videos or moving sidewalks here, though. To find out more about these facilities, contact the U.S. Hockey Hall of Fame, P.O. Box 657, Eveleth, Minn. 55734. Phone (218) 744-5167. Or get in touch with the Hockey Hall of Fame, Exhibition Place, Toronto, Ontario, Canada M6K3C3. Phone (416) 595-1345.

PROFESSIONAL ALL-STAR GAMES

Sure, you want to go to the baseball All-Star game. Who doesn't? Or maybe basketball is your sport, so you'd rather see the NBA All-Star game. Or wouldn't it be great to take your kids to see *all* the All-Star games one year? Now *there's* a sports fan's fantasy come true!

Unfortunately, unless you're one of the lucky few who have inside connections, or are a season ticket holder in the city where an All-Star game is held, you aren't likely to get tickets to these super-popular events. For all three major sports—basketball, baseball and hockey—the tickets are offered first to the season ticket holders in the hosting city, then the NBA, NHL, or major baseball leagues take the remainder of the tickets and distribute them to sponsors of the game. Are there any tickets left over after that? Very few. Unlike the Super Bowl, for which a ticket lottery is held each year, there simply aren't enough tickets to the All-Star games, so the general public is generally out of luck. You can write to the NBA, NHL, or major baseball leagues and request tickets—but don't hold your breath.

OTHER HALLS OF FAME

Almost every sport has a Hall of Fame to immortalize its great athletes, although not all such museums are as elaborate or sophisticated as the ones described earlier in this chapter. Sports ranging from bowling to horseracing have small museums honoring their athletes. To find out about a Hall of Fame for your favorite sport, contact the appropriate national organization for that sport.

TENNIS AND GOLF

For a family with older children and a passion for tennis, the ultimate fantasy is to be holding tickets to the U.S. Open, one of the premiere tennis championships in the world.

To obtain tickets to the U.S. Open, which is held around Labor Day each year in Flushing Meadow, New York, contact the National Tennis Center, Flushing Meadow, Corona Park, Flushing, N.Y. 11368. Or you can reach them by phone at (718) 271-5100. When you call or write, you'll be put on the mailing list for ticket announcements, which come in the spring. Tickets are sold on a first-come, first-served basis, so don't delay. Send in your ticket request immediately, and chances are good that you'll get seats for the day or days you want.

A golfing clan dreams of finding itself at the U.S. Open golf tournament. Tickets usually go on sale for the next year immediately following the Open in the current year. There are about 40,000 tickets available for each tournament day, and traditionally, they haven't been too difficult to get—though in 1990, all tickets for the 1991 U.S. Open were sold out within three weeks. The tournament is held in a different location each year on Father's Day weekend in June, and tickets are sold directly through the sponsoring country club. For information about location and tickets, contact the U.S. Golf Association, USGA Golf House, P.O. Box 708, Far Hills, N.J. 07931-0708. Phone (201) 234-2300.

Just for the record, if you've ever entertained thoughts of attending the Masters golf tournament, forget it. The Masters, held at Augusta National Golf Club in Georgia each year, has been over-subscribed for so long that they closed their ticket mailing lists—in 1971! Since then, only people who were already subscribers to the tournament have been able to attend.

OLYMPIC GOLD

Every few years the Olympics come blasting out of nowhere to generate enormous enthusiasm for a wide variety of sports among normally oblivious television viewers around the globe. Figure skating, gymnastics, equestrian events, swimming, cycling, the four-man bobsled, field hockey, ice hockey, archery, ski-jumping and luge—to name just a few—are among the sports which many American families follow only sporadically or not at all, until an Olympic year comes along. And then, bam! It's Olympic mania-time. Families sit glued to their television sets, soaking up all the details and excitement and wishing that it didn't have to end.

Well, guess what? It doesn't. Competitions in these "Olympic" sports are held several times every year, at various locations throughout the United States. You don't have to depend on network television coverage to quench your enthusiasm for Olympic sports. There are dozens of ways to stay in touch with what's happening in them during the time between the Olympics—and there are dozens of related family adventures you can take.

For starters, you can find out about the major competitions in your favorite Olympic sports, and then make plans to attend in person. There's nothing like watching the annual U.S. Figure Skating Championships, especially in an Olympic year, when a skater's performance at the championships will determine whether he or she makes the Olympic team. You'll see top-level athletes of the caliber of Debbie Thomas, Jill Trenary, Brian Boitano and Scott Hamilton. During the Junior competition, held at the same time, you might see an unknown 11-year-old taking her first steps toward an Olympics four or eight years down the road.

Other opportunities abound. Would you like to attend an international fencing competition, or watch the up-and-coming American track and field stars compete in the NCAA Championships? Or maybe you'd like to check out the bobsled run in Lake Placid, or watch your favorite athletes train at an official Olympic Training Center.

All of these adventures are possible, and are encouraged by the U.S. Olympic Committee, which is headquartered in Colorado Springs, Colorado. The Public Relations office of the USOC maintains lists of schedules and information about each of the Olympic sports and is happy to answer all kinds of inquiries from the public. Contact the USOC P.R. Office to ask about events, or to find out how various Olympic rules are developed, or even to find out the chances of curling—an unusual Scottish game played on ice with a stone and a broom—being added to the Olympic lineup. Write to the U.S. Olympic Committee, Public Information Division, 1750 East Boulder Street, Colorado Springs, Colo. 80909. Or phone (719) 632-5551.

You can also contact the governing bodies for the sports you are interested in. The national governing body (NGB) for each sport can provide you with an annual schedule of the sport's major competitions ranging from national championships to regional age-group competitions, and including locations, dates and ticket information. For instance, if you are interested in gymnastics, you would contact the U.S. Gymnastics Federation (USGF), located in Indianapolis, Indiana. For 1990, the federation would have sent you the schedule for seven major gymnastics events, five of which were held in the United States, including the National Championships in Denver. Tickets for that event were available through the ticket offices of the specific facility where the event was held, which was the Denver Coliseum. But unless you lived in Denver, or you contacted the USGF, you might never have known that a major gymnastics competition was being held.

The national governing bodies for all Olympic sports are listed in the Appendix, beginning on page 133. When you contact an NGB, you might also ask whether there is a magazine for that sport to which you can subscribe. Some of the more popular sports offer magazines by subscription only through the NGB. For instance, there is *Skating Magazine* available from the U.S. Figure Skating Association, with articles about America's premiere individual skaters, promising new pairs skaters, recent competitions, and so forth. Subscribing to these publications is a great way to find out about the athletes you might be seeing in person during your family's trip to a championship competition.

OLYMPIC TRIALS

How are the players selected for the U.S. ice hockey team? How are teams chosen for the four-man bobsled? Where can you go to see the Olympic trials for the 100-meter track event, or the high-jump or the hurdles?

The timing and methods for selecting athletes vary widely from one sport to another. Divers, for instance, are usually selected only two months before the Olympics, through a series of Olympic trials. Skaters don't have Olympic trials. They are selected following the U.S. Championships that take place in the Olympic year, with most of the weight being placed on their performances in the championship competition. Gymnasts, on the other hand, are selected almost a year in advance, based on a number of factors, including the U.S. Championships and Olympic trials. And Alpine skiers are often selected at the last minute, only a few weeks before the Winter Olympics begin.

But one way or another, each NGB must select the athletes who will represent the United States at the Olympics. And in many cases, you can be there when the decisions are being made. All you need to do is contact the NGB for the sport you're interested in, and ask about Olympic trials. If they don't hold trials, they'll tell you which competition is used as a qualifying event instead. Tickets for Olympic trials are often sold through the NGBs directly; if not, the NGB can tell you how to obtain them.

By the way, all track and field events, such as the 100-meter, the high-jump and the hurdles are officially dubbed "Athletics" and are governed by The Athletics Congress. See the Appendix for a complete address.

OLYMPIC TRAINING CENTERS

Another golden opportunity to see Olympic stars up close is to visit one of the Olympic Training Centers. The biggest and busiest center is in Colorado Springs, Colorado. Free guided tours are given every day of the week, and offer you the chance to see some of the athletes who live and train at this location year round. The training center is a state-of-the-art facility which houses, among other things, a unique swimming flume that can generate currents of various speeds and can simulate the effect on a swimmer of altitudes from sea level to 7,000 feet. There are also five gymnasiums, an outdoor track, sports medicine facilities and a center for rifle and pistol shooting. Near the center there is a USOC-operated velodrome for track cycling events.

Your free tour of the Olympic Training Center lasts about an hour and a half, and includes a visit to the gift shop and a film. For recorded information about the Olympic Training Center's current schedule of events, call the OTC hotline, open 24 hours a day, at (719) 578-4644. For more information, call (719) 578-4618. The Olympic Training Center is located at 1776 East Boulder Street, Colorado Springs, Colo. 80909.

Although figure skaters do not train at the official Olympic Training Center in Colorado Springs, they are often in residence at the Broadmoor World Arena, which is located across town. Training sessions at the Broadmoor are also free and are usually open to the public, and the arena is happy to tell you which skaters are expected to be there during any

upcoming time period. For a real thrill, you might want to arrive in time to hit the ice yourself during the afternoon public skating session, then hang around to watch the top-level skaters who usually train in the early evening. For more information contact the Broadmoor World Arena, 1 Lake Avenue, Colorado Springs, Colo. 80906. Phone (719) 634-7711.

The Olympic Training Center in Lake Placid, New York, soon intends to offer free guided tours of its facilities, which were renovated and expanded in 1990. The center itself has a dormitory to house athletes who are in training for basketball, team handball, wrestling, luge, bobsled, skiing and the biathlon. In addition, there is a sports medicine complex, a gymnasium, a weight room, a cafeteria for athletes only and a gift shop. For more information, contact the Olympic Training Center, 421 Old Military Road, Lake Placid, N.Y. 12946. Phone (518) 523-2600.

But the real attractions in Lake Placid are the winter sports facilities that are owned and maintained by the New York Olympic Regional Development Authority. Site of the 1980 Winter Olympic Games, Lake Placid boasts the only bobsled and luge runs in the country, plus a host of other winter sports facilities including alpine and cross-country ski trails and an Olympic-sized speed-skating oval. All are open to the public, so for the price of a $20 ticket, you can hop on a bobsled and take a thrilling ride down the same track used by the U.S. Olympic bobsled team. If you're wondering about safety, don't worry. The public bobsled rides are driven by an experienced driver, and they depart from the half-mile point rather than from the top of the track. Luge rides are $10 per person and also depart from midway down the track. Public skating is available indoors and outdoors on the Olympic speed-skating oval, and the ski slopes are open as well. If you're more a winter sports spectator than a participant, you can come to Lake Placid to watch the World Cup Ski Jumping competitions in December, or one of the various international freestyle competitions held there every year.

For more information, contact the New York Olympic Regional Development Authority, Olympic Center, Lake Placid, N.Y. 12946. Phone (518) 523-1655.

As this book went to press, another Olympic Training Center was under construction in San Diego, California. Thanks to the mild climate in San Diego, this facility will be the first year-round, multi-sport complex in the country. Facilities will be geared toward outdoor sports such as archery, athletics, canoeing and kayaking, cycling, field hockey, rowing, soccer, synchronized swimming and water polo. When completed, the training center may offer tours and/or be a source of further information about Olympic athletes. So stay tuned . . . .

U.S. OLYMPIC FESTIVAL

Unbeknownst to many, in 1978 the USOC began sponsoring an Olympic-like competition as another opportunity for U.S. athletes to compete in Olympic sports in non-Olympic years. Originally called the National Sports Festival, the name was changed to the U.S. Olympic Festival in 1985 "to help the public identify the Festival's role in the overall Olympic Movement." The Festival is staged every non-Olympic summer in a different city, and it continues to grow—often producing sell-out or standing-room-only crowds for even the more obscure sports such as table tennis, fencing and team handball. Attending the Festival is a terrific way to get in on the excitement of Olympic sports.

What will you see if you attend the Olympic Festival? Legendary athletes like Mary Lou Retton, Carl Lewis, Linda Fratianne, Florence Griffith Joyner, Greg Louganis and Mike Eruzione all appeared at the festival one time or another, some making their major debuts there, so you can count on seeing a mix of young world-class athletes in the making, as well as superstars at the pinnacle of their careers.

For more information and a schedule of Festival cities for upcoming years, contact the U.S. Olympic Committee. Tickets for the Festival are not sold through the USOC, however. They are handled by a local organizing committee in the sponsoring city. The USOC can direct you to the appropriate agency.

OLYMPIC HALL OF FAME

Don't pack your bags—it's not built yet. But as of this writing, a U.S. Olympic Hall of Fame is in the works. Fund-raising is underway, and more than half of the $20 million goal has been attained, and 150 acres of land in Colorado Springs, Colorado, have been donated for the facility.

In the meantime, Olympic athletes are being inducted each year, becoming Hall of Famers despite the fact that there's no physical hall. The first inductees, in 1983, Jesse Owens, Jim Thorpe, Muhammed Ali, Dick Button, Johnny Weissmuller, Eric Heiden, Mark Spitz and 13 others. In the years since, the number of Hall of Famers has grown to include more than 125 athletes whose contributions to their sports are internationally recognized. In addition, there are eight Special Contributors—people such as Avery Brundage, Robert J. Kane, Jim McKay and Roone Arledge who have made lasting contributions to the Olympic movement.

It should be a great place to visit with your kids! Watch for it, or better yet, send a tax-deductible contribution to the Colorado Amateur Sports Corporation, 12 East Boulder, Colorado Springs, Colo. 80903, and help to get the Hall of Fame built.

OLYMPIC FEVER: GETTING YOUR KIDS PSYCHED

Given the media coverage and attention that most Olympic sports receive, it isn't hard to get most kids excited about the Olympics during an Olympic year. But what if your children are too young to be aware of the Olympics? Or what if they don't share your enthusiasm and reverence for a particular sport?

The answer is probably waiting for you at the local video store in the form of an Olympic highlights tape. Highlights tapes are slickly-produced videos with enough pulsating music, flag waving and crowd-cheering to get any kid at least a little bit pumped up about the glamour and glory of the Olympic tradition. You might also rent a movie about past Olympic competitions—"Chariots of Fire," for instance. As any classroom teacher knows, it's always a good idea to provide a little background information before going on a field trip. And your "field trip" to watch an Olympic sporting event is no different. Your kids will enjoy it more if you can convey your enthusiasm to them and educate them a little bit about the sport before you go.

WIDE OPEN SPACES

One of the most exhilarating feelings you can have on any family adventure is the sudden recognition that the United States is indeed a vast, beautiful country. This chapter covers horseback riding, bicycle touring and skiing—three excellent ways to get a different perspective on our extraordinary landscape. In all three sports adventures, you'll confront the wide open spaces of America and find yourself dazzled by the feeling of freedom, filled with a sense of wonder at the enormity of the countryside and thrill of moving from place to place under your own power.

ON HORSEBACK: DUDE RANCHES, GUEST FARMS AND MORE

A hundred years ago, when the Wild West was really wild, city folks sometimes travelled westward and paid hefty fees to stay as guests at working cattle ranches. The guests soon came to be called "dudes," a term that was not entirely complimentary, referring to the fastidious way the Eastern men dressed. Nonetheless, the tradition persisted, and the ranches became known as dude ranches.

Today, the dude ranch experience is unique among family adventure vacations. Often you travel a great distance from your home to get to the unspoiled wilderness area in which the ranch is situated and, as you travel, each leg of your journey requires a less-sophisticated form of transportation. For example, you might fly on a major airline to Denver, then transfer to a smaller airline for a hop to a tiny airport in a remote Montana city, then travel by car or bus for an hour or more to the ranch. Once you've reached your destination, you'll find that modern means of transportation are no longer appropriate at all! To see the countryside and to explore the raw beauty of the jagged mountains, you'll need to travel on horseback—or on foot. The mountainous terrain is too steep, too narrow and sometimes too treacherous to admit any motorized vehicle. The journey into the wilderness setting alone will transport you and your family into a world of adventure, rich with the atmosphere of another time and place.

Today dude ranches offer a rustic western atmosphere tempered with

a nod to modern conveniences and, sometimes, the creature comforts that resort guests often seek. How many creature comforts, and how much of a resort feeling you get, will depend on the ranch you choose.

Most dude ranches are set up for week-long visits only, although a few will accommodate guests on weekends or for shorter mid-week stays. The standard arrangement calls for you to arrive on Sunday, often being met at the nearest airport by ranch personnel. Sunday is spent settling in and getting acquainted with the ranch. You can enjoy many of the ranch activities—except riding, as it is "horses' day off." Monday morning the wranglers will begin assessing your riding experience and assigning horses. Don't worry if you've never been on a horse before—most guests at dude ranches are "tenderfeet." Many ranches assign you a horse on the first day, and if you like the choice, you may keep the same horse for the entire week. Typically, wrangler-led trail rides are scheduled twice daily, one in the morning and one in the afternoon, each lasting about two hours. And you *must* ride with the wranglers. For your own safety and the safety of the horses, you are not permitted to ride off into the sunset by yourself.

As the week progresses, most ranches offer longer trail rides, either an all-day ride or a ride up to a mountain lake for a cookout lunch. Overnight pack trips are usually available for a surcharge. On pack trips, you and your family ride into the mountains with staff members, accompanied by pack animals that carry the camping gear. When you arrive at the campsite, the staff sets up camp, pitches the tents, makes a fire and cooks dinner while you explore the countryside. You sleep in tents under the stars, often listening to a howling coyote as you drift off to sleep. The next day you ride back to the ranch, perhaps taking a different trail on your return.

Most ranches offer the full horseback riding package to children ages six and up. Younger children are led on pony rides around the meadows nearer to the ranch, but may not join the trail rides. A supervised children's program is often included in the package rate, with programs tailored to different age groups. Games, crafts, children's cookouts, teen wilderness hikes, swimming and riding lessons are all standard. Your children's day won't be completely structured and scheduled, but at some ranches, the time children spend apart from parents exceeds the family time spent together. At many ranches, for instance, children are required to take their meals at an earlier hour, with the counselors, so that adults can enjoy a more peaceful meal. So read the brochures carefully and ask questions in advance. That way you'll find a ranch that suits your family's inclinations.

And speaking of meals . . . families with picky eaters should make extensive inquiries about the food before signing up for a week-long stay in a remote area, miles and miles from the fast-food chains! Most ranches offer only one entree at each meal, and sometimes it can be quite exotic. One ranch serves 57 varieties of local specialty—elk meat—all week long. Elk is even incorporated into the spaghetti sauce! Even a ranch's more standard offerings may not appeal to the six-year-old palate, in which case you might make sure your accommodations include a kitchen or refrigerator in your suite. That way, you can always have unlimited supplies of peanut butter or cereal. But bring it from home, as the nearest store may be 100 miles away!

Since many dude and guest ranches are located within striking distance of one or more of the national parks, you may want to plan a vacation which includes a week at a dude ranch followed by a few days or more spent on your own. If your vacation time is limited to one week, consider one of the ranches that are directly adjacent to a park. Some ranches will help you arrange day trips to the neighboring national parks as part of your stay.

Other things you need to know about dude ranches:

▶ Rates almost always are on the American Plan; i.e., inclusive of all meals. You generally pay one package price for everything—meals, lodging, riding and all activities. Read the ranch's printed material carefully, however. Some ranches automatically add 15 percent for gratuities on to your bill—whether you wish to tip the staff or not. Tipping the ranch hands is expected, however. The standard tip is 15 percent of the total bill.

▶ There are usually no telephones or TVs in the guest rooms.

▶ Boots or shoes with a definite heel are a necessity for horseback riding. You might think that tennis shoes would suffice, but the ranch owners won't agree with you. Plan to bring boots, or buy them in town en route to the ranch. A few ranches have extra boots on hand which they will rent or lend you for the week. Be sure to ask in advance.

▶ Western hats are also a necessity on horseback. Why? Because when a gust of wind lifts your hat off your head, the strings on a western hat will keep it from blowing away. Hats and sundries are usually available in the gift shop at the ranch, although boots are more often not.

▶ Remember that horseback riding is not risk-free. The animals are large and the trails can be steep enough to cause a horse to stumble. Even old ranch hands occasionally go down with their mounts. One staff cook on an overnight pack trip went down with his horse recently, because the horse had suddenly decided to roll in the mud! Even though the wranglers at many ranches are trained in first-aid and/or emergency care, you will probably be required to sign a release form on arrival, exempting the ranch owners and staff from any responsibility in case of injury.

▶ Some of the best ranches are rather small, accepting only about 35–40 guests per week. Since the return rate among guests is high, it's often necessary to make reservations well in advance. If you want to combine your ranch experience with a visit to a national park that includes staying in the popular park facilities, you must begin planning a summer trip in the middle of winter.

▶ Most ranches will suggest what clothing you should bring, either in the brochures or in a letter sent upon receipt of a reservation deposit. Heed their advice. If they say you won't need formal clothes, they mean it. At most ranches, you'll be happiest with jeans, shirts and sweaters.

▶ Getting to your destination will almost always entail changing planes, or renting a car, taking a train or at least paying a surcharge for airport-to-ranch transportation. After all, you're trying to get away from civilization and that takes some doing!

One last note: Dude ranches often double as ski resorts in winter. The pastures and mountain trails making excellent cross-country skiing trails. So when you're planning a winter family sports adventure, consider the ranch where you spent your last summer vacation.

Following is a selection of some of the best dude ranches in the West, chosen for their superior facilities and the quality of the accommodations, the comprehensive nature of the riding program, the availability of other recreational activities and the excellence of the childrens' program. Also listed are two Eastern ranches which offer horseback riding vacations at especially affordable rates. For more information about other dude ranches, contact the Department of Tourism in the state you wish to visit.

VISTA VERDE GUEST RANCH
Steamboat Springs, Colorado

Set amidst some of the most majestic scenery in the Rocky Mountains, this small, first-class guest ranch offers an ideal escape from civilization without abandoning the basic comforts that make family vacations more enjoyable. The ranch accepts no more than 35–40 guests at a time—just enough to provide a congenial collection of compatriots for a vacation that is both stimulating and relaxed. Spruce trees are everywhere, towering overhead as part of the cool green landscape from which Vista Verde takes its name, and horizontally stacked to form the authentic Main Lodge and log guest cabins, all of which are nestled among bubbling streams. Thanks to the greenery, you won't find a lot of dust, which is often an unpleasant feature at guest ranches. Instead, there are meadows filled with wildflowers, unforgettable views of the Rocky Mountains, and cool starry nights. Wildlife is abundant on the ranch's 600 acres; elk, deer, fox, coyotes, beavers, porcupines and golden and bald eagles populate the countryside.

The ranch is owned and operated by Frank and Winton Brophy, transplanted Easterners who "went west" to find a quieter, more peaceful existence than was available in the suburbs of New York City. As a result, the atmosphere at Vista Verde is less western than wilderness, with the emphasis on family, friends and an appreciation of the surrounding natural beauty.

At Vista Verde, you are assigned a horse for the week. The horse is chosen according to your riding ability. Morning and afternoon trail rides, led by a wrangler, are organized in groups of four or five. Riding lessons are always available, and children are given special attention. The ranch even keeps two miniature horses, so that small children may enjoy the experience of brushing and currying a mount. There are also plenty of ducks, lambs, peacocks and pygmy goats to pet and feed.

In addition to riding, the ranch offers rock climbing, fishing, a full-day whitewater float trip on the upper Colorado River, square dancing, a gold-panning expedition, hay rides, games, lake swimming, a children's program, rodeo admissions, gymkhana (a participatory rodeo for guests), hot tub/sauna and an exercise room—all included in the weekly package rate. For additional fees, you may also arrange a hot air balloon ride, a mountain bike tour, an overnight pack trip and sailing, golf, hunting or fly fishing instruction.

Vista Verde is one of many guest ranches which become ski resorts in winter. Of course the same gorgeous scenery is right at your doorstep in winter, except that it's covered with four feet of snow. Sleigh rides, snowshoeing, ice-fishing and excellent cross-country skiing are all part of the winter package. Downhill skiing is available in nearby Steamboat Springs.

LOCATION: Vista Verde is surrounded by the Routt National Forest and the Mount Zirkel Wilderness Area. It is four hours by car northwest of Denver, 25 miles north of Steamboat Springs. The Elk River, well-known for its trout, borders the ranch. Yellowstone National Park and the Grand Teton National Parks are about 450 miles northwest.

MEALS AND ACCOMMODATIONS: Each cabin has a cozy living room with wood-burning fireplace, full kitchen and bath and deck or porch over-looking a stream. Cabin sizes range from one to three bedrooms. The kitchens are a nice extra, especially for families with small children or picky eaters, but don't plan on spending your vacation cooking, as the rates include all meals. Homegrown fresh vegetables, homemade breads, pastries, pies and large portions of barbecued steak, chicken and fish are common at Vista Verde. The food is attractively served either in the main dining room or outdoors near the barbecue pit.

RATES: Weekly rates are per person, including three meals a day, airport transfers and all activities listed above. Adults, $1,200 per week; children under 12 years, $950 per week; children under 6 years, $850 per week.

FOR MORE INFORMATION: Contact Vista Verde Guest Ranch, Box 465, Steamboat Springs, Colo. 80477. Phone (800) 526-RIDE or (303) 879-3858.

LONE MOUNTAIN RANCH
Big Sky, Montana

Superior food, proximity to Yellowstone National Park and outstanding trout fishing opportunities are features which set this ranch apart from many others. Situated in a secluded valley of Gallatin Canyon, with the snow-capped Spanish Peaks as a backdrop, the ranch is less than one hour from Yellowstone National Park. For families who want unlimited horseback riding in an unspoiled wilderness setting, combined with a visit to Yellowstone, Lone Mountain Ranch is an ideal choice.

Twice-daily trail rides are standard at Lone Mountain Ranch, along with several all-day rides scheduled each week. At least once a week, the wranglers transport the horses by trailer to a remote location so that guests can explore other aspects of the countryside. (Guests are taken to and from the location by bus or another ranch vehicle.) Lessons for beginners are included in the package, while advanced lessons are available at a surcharge. Children under six are allowed only on short, wrangler-led pony rides around the ranch.

Among the special activities offered by the ranch are wilderness walks led by naturalists well-versed in such subjects as bird watching, wildlife photography, Indian trails, geology and star-gazing. An all-day tour of Yellowstone National Park, led by one of Lone Mountain's naturalists, is another option and promises to be a more rewarding experience than any self-guided tours of the park. Overnight horseback trips into Yellowstone can also be arranged for an additional fee.

For serious fly fishing enthusiasts, Lone Mountain offers a variety of special package vacations, at separate rates. These packages include guided wading trips, horseback fishing trips, drift boat fishing and float tube fishing. All fishing programs are endorsed by Orvis, a premiere manufacturer of fly fishing gear. Combination rates are available for families in which one family member wants to fish while other family members are at home on the range.

LOCATION: The ranch is located northwest of Yellowstone National Park, less than one hour by car from the park. The nearest airport is in Bozeman, Montana, about 40 miles north of the ranch.

MEALS AND ACCOMMODATIONS: Cozy, well-maintained log cabins with one or two bedrooms, wood-burning fireplaces, modern bathrooms and front porches are the rule here. The food is noteworthy, having received notice in such publications as *Bon Appetit, Esquire* and the *New York Times.* The owners like to say the food is "ranch cooking with a gourmet flair," and they pride themselves on their health-conscious approach as well.

RATES: Weekly rates include all meals, six days of horseback riding, airport shuttle, one basic riding lesson, children's programs, evening programs, on-ranch naturalist programs, and barbecues. Adults, $798 per double occupancy in a one room cabin; children ages 6-12, $497-$735, depending on number of adults. Reduced rates are available for younger children and additional persons sharing a cabin. Rates are slightly higher for larger cabins, but discounts are available when larger cabins are shared by two families.

FOR MORE INFORMATION: Contact Lone Mountain Ranch, P.O. Box 69, Big Sky, Mont. 59716. Phone (406) 995-4644.

AVERILL'S FLATHEAD LAKE LODGE AND DUDE RANCH
Bigfork, Montana

If you're looking for an authentic western dude ranch atmosphere, enhanced by a more complete selection of outdoor recreation activities than dude ranches ordinarily offer, you might want to try Averill's. This famous ranch and lodge, located on 2,000 acres in the Rocky Mountains, has been a family-run operation since 1945. The Averill brothers (there are eight of them, four of whom own the ranch) pride themselves on offering the largest variety of activities at one all-inclusive price. The claim is difficult to dispute. Complete with tennis courts, a heated pool, many water sport activities—including sailing, canoeing, fishing and water skiing on the clean, clear Flathead Lake—and, of course, horseback riding, the ranch comes close to attaining resort status without sacrificing the western flavor that sent you searching for a dude ranch in the first place.

Of particular appeal to children is a ranch-supervised overnight camp-out in tepees near the lake. Other children's activities available include arts and crafts, and horseback rides, but full-day childcare is *not* included in the rate. The rates are extremely reasonable for children under four, partly because there is no program for this age group. The ranch will recommend local babysitters, however, if you wish to hire someone yourself for part of your visit.

Both children and adults can enjoy a day trip to nearby Glacier National Park, where the wildlife sightings include elk, bear, deer, bald eagles and a wide variety of other birds. Weekly rodeo competitions are also a favorite among ranch guests, who may participate at the end of their stay to show off their newly acquired skills.

LOCATION: The ranch is situated in the northwest corner of Montana, just south of Glacier National Park. Kalispell is the nearest city with an airport.

MEALS AND ACCOMMODATIONS: Barbecued buffalo, roast pig and fresh salmon are among the specialties at the ranch. You can also expect more traditional hearty fare of prime rib, steak, flapjacks and bacon, home-made breads, pastries and pies, often made with local Montana berries. The ranch accommodates up to 100 guests at a time, with families staying in rustic cabins, while singles and couples occupy rooms in the lodges.

RATES: Weekly rates, from Sunday to Sunday, include all meals, lodging, horseback riding twice daily, rodeo events, cookouts, water sports, use of sailboats, canoes, fishing gear and boats, pool, tennis courts, volleyball and all other ranch facilities. Adults, $1,085 per person, double occupancy; teens, $869; children ages 4-12, $697; children under 4, $96. There is an additional charge for pack trips, whitewater float trips and wilderness fishing.

FOR MORE INFORMATION: Contact Averill's Flathead Lake Lodge, Box 248, Bigfork, Mont. 59911. Phone (406) 837-4391.

TUMBLING RIVER RANCH
Grant, Colorado

At 9,200 feet above sea level, Tumbling River Ranch is truly a Rocky Mountain high experience. Even in July, the temperature rarely goes above 75°F, and mountain nights are cool enough to require a sweater or jacket—or better yet, a blazing fire in your own snug cabin. The trails are steep, the scenery as rarified as the air. (Allergy sufferers will love this location, because it's too high for hay fever plants, so the breathing is easy!) And if 9,200 feet isn't high enough for you, you can hop into a four-wheel drive vehicle and take a trip up to Geneva, an old mining town above the timberline.

The history of the Rockies, and of the Indian tribes who once populated the area, is in evidence everywhere here. On arrival, you'll be struck by the age and authenticity of the ranch buildings. The Pueblo, one of two larger guest lodges, was originally the mountain home of Adolph Coors' daughter. Built in the 1920s by Taos Indians, who hand-carved the decorative beams, this extraordinary structure is filled with Indian artifacts and western antiques. There are seven guest rooms in the Pueblo, each with its own fireplace. A dining room and huge living room overlook a pond stocked with trout.

The layout of Tumbling River Ranch affords the guests a sense of privacy and community at the same time. The Pueblo is about half a mile away from the main ranch house and assorted guest cabins. A pleasant walk along the "tumbling river," which is officially named Geneva Creek, connects the two areas of the ranch. Together, the two lodge buildings and cabins can accommodate about a dozen families at any one time.

One of the biggest herd of big-horn sheep on the continent can often be seen from the dining room of the upper ranch house. Elk, deer, mountain goats, bear and beaver are also native inhabitants. But you *won't* find poisonous snakes here. According to ranch owners Mary Dale and Jim Gordon, the altitude keeps them away.

Ranch activities at Tumbling River include the usual assortment of trail rides, unlimited riding instruction, and an end-of-week rodeo for guests. The snowcapped peaks of the Continental Divide are within riding distance of the ranch. But what really makes this ranch special is its emphasis on exploring the countryside for bits of Western history—an old mine or an abandoned trapper's cabin in the mountains, for instance. Children ages six and older are welcome to participate fully in the trail rides, either in children's groups or with adults.

For an additional fee, whitewater rafting and overnight horseback trips may be arranged.

LOCATION: The ranch is 50 miles southwest of Denver, with Pike's Peak visible to the south. The Pike National Forest surrounds the ranch property.

MEALS AND ACCOMMODATIONS: Cookouts are common at Tumbling River Ranch, and dinners typically feature steak, turkey, prime rib, trout or barbecued ribs. Guest rooms vary from individual guest bedrooms with fireplace and bath, to two-bathroom, two-bedroom suites in the Pueblo lodge. The guest cabins consist of two units which can be occupied separately or opened to adjoin. Each unit has its own bath and fireplace.

RATES: Weekly rates are per person, double occupancy for July and August, and include all meals, horseback riding, four-wheel-drive trips, children's programs for 3-year-olds and up, fishing, heated pool, sauna and evening activities. Adults, $1,000; children ages 6–12, $800; ages 3–6 $700; children under 3, $300. Rates for the full program are lower in June; significantly lower in spring and fall, when the air is even cooler and evening activities are not offered.

FOR MORE INFORMATION: Contact Tumbling River Ranch, Grant, Colo. 80448. Phone (303) 838-5981.

C LAZY U RANCH
Granby, Colorado

This well-known resort-type ranch receives the highest ratings from both the Mobil Travel Guide and AAA—five stars and five diamonds, respectively. Expect to find top-notch rooms on the order of first-class hotel rooms, exceptional meals and attentive service here. You can also expect larger crowds and a real resort atmosphere. In addition to daily horseback rides tailored to your ability, there is a full complement of recreation activities available: tennis courts, skeet shooting, indoor racquetball, swimming pool, whirlpool, sauna, paddle boats and pond, lake and stream fishing. Evening entertainment includes square dancing and staff talent shows, as well as western swing dances with a live band.

Two separate programs accommodate children ages 3–5 and 6–12. Children six and up may participate fully in the horseback riding program. Children under three are accepted at the ranch only during specified weeks each summer.

In winter, C Lazy U Ranch becomes a first-class cross-country ski resort, offering a full range of winter sports activities.

LOCATION: situated on some 2,500 acres 8,300 feet above sea level in the Colorado Rockies, the ranch is less than two hours by car from Denver. Rocky Mountain National Park is about 10 miles away.

MEALS AND ACCOMMODATIONS: Lunch is always served at the pool in the summer, with a soup/salad/sandwich bar available in addition to the main menu. Dinner entrees include chicken Waikiki, rib eye and New York strip steaks and salmon Teriyaki. Children are offered simpler fare such as fried chicken, hamburgers and grilled cheese sandwiches. You should know that children eat breakfast with their parents, but eat lunch and dinner separately and are not allowed in the dining area during adult lunches and dinners. Guest rooms vary in size, and are located in a variety of smaller buildings surrounding the main lodge.

RATES: Rates vary based on number of people, number of rooms, type, and location of accommodations. Children ages six and over are charged the full adult rate; children three to five receive a $200 per week discount. At peak season, the weekly rate, including all meals and activities, ranges from $815–$1445 per person.

FOR MORE INFORMATION: Contact C Lazy U Ranch, P.O. Box 378, Granby, Colo. 80446. Phone (303) 887-3344.

ROCKING HORSE RANCH
Highland, New York

Although rugged scenery, clean mountain air and a dramatically different lifestyle attract families to a dude ranch, it isn't necessary to head for Colorado or Montana to find all that, and a lot of horseback riding to boot. The Rocking Horse Ranch, easily the closest thing to a western ranch experience east of the Mississippi, can be found a short 90 minutes drive from New York City. There are 500 beautiful acres of mountains and orchards on which to ride, and enough additional activities to keep you occupied when the saddle sores begin to take hold. Among the offerings are archery, water skiing, paddle and row boats, fishing, miniature golf, hay rides, tennis, indoor and outdoor swimming, handball, horseshoes, croquet, a fitness gym and more. A supervised children's program is also included in the package.

The ranch successfully combines western decor with contemporary amenities to produce a "best of both worlds" feeling. For instance, western wagon wheels abound, both inside and out. But the meals are decidedly more eastern resort-oriented than chuck wagon style. In fact, this ranch is one of the few to offer a choice of entrees at meals. Selections may include shrimp scampi, chicken Kiev, filet mignon, mussels marinara, veal marsala and blackened swordfish, along with a salad bar, seasonal fruits and assorted desserts.

The weekly rates at Rocking Horse Ranch are significantly lower than those at similar ranches in the West. And with daily and weekend rates available, this ranch offers families an opportunity to try a dude ranch adventure without investing a small fortune.

LOCATION: In the heart of the Hudson River Valley, just outside of New Paltz, New York.

MEALS AND ACCOMMODATIONS: There is a rotating menu at the ranch, with extensive choices offered nightly. All meals are served on an all-you-can-eat basis. Guest rooms, located either in the main lodge or the adjacent Oklahoma building, are large and comfortable, with private baths, air conditioning, telephones and cable TV. Decor is more like a motel than a dude ranch, and larger rooms or suites, called ranchettes, have sitting areas, refrigerators and coffee-makers.

RATES: Rates vary seasonally, with special packages available for holiday weeks and weekends. On stays of two nights or more, there is a meal charge of $21 per night for children. Rates include all activities and three meals per day. Sample rate for a spring visit, per person, double occupancy in a room large enough to accommodate additional children: Adults, $105 per night, $485 per week; children $21 daily meal charge.

FOR MORE INFORMATION: Contact Rocking Horse Ranch, Highland, N.Y. 12528. Phone (800) 647-2624 or (914) 691-2927.

HONEY LANE FARM
Peterborough, New Hampshire

Honey Lane Farm is not a dude ranch at all, but rather a unique family-owned facility for horseback riding in the picturesque rolling countryside of New Hampshire. For most of the summer, the farm is a horsemanship camp for children, which teaches English riding skills rather than Western, in an indoor arena and outdoors on woodland trails. But in spring and fall, and for one week in June, the farm is open to families for weekend or week-long horsemanship vacations. The week-long vacations are run like a family camp, with the emphasis on learning all about horses, not just how to ride. There are lectures on general horse care, feeding, health and stable management, as well as hands-on grooming projects, daily riding lessons, videos, trail rides and more. Spring and fall weekends are less structured and more relaxed. The program is a great quickie seminar for parents of children who already know how to ride, or for families who are seriously considering buying a horse. Seasoned horse people are often guests here, drawn in part by the fact that Honey Lane will stable your horse if you choose to bring your own mount. But everyone is welcome, even dabblers and nonriders. Some spring and fall weekend trips are aptly called "Learn-to-Ride" weekends, which should give you an idea of the program. In the fall, you get the additional pleasure of taking in the breathtaking New England fall foliage.

Owners Aline and Al Coutu are warm, outgoing people who happily extend themselves to make your vacation a success. Having chosen to abandon "traditional" careers in favor of the horse farm they love, they now pride themselves on maintaining an excellent facility. Since much of their time is spent teaching young people to ride during summer camp sessions, they are highly skilled in working with children.

LOCATION: The farm is located on 100 woodland acres in southwestern New Hampshire, between Dublin and Peterborough, near Mt. Monadnock, about 75 miles northwest of Boston.

MEALS AND ACCOMMODATIONS: There are two types of accommodations at Honey Lane Farm. The bunkhouse is rustic; there is no indoor bathroom (only an outdoor toilet) and you are required to bring your own towels and sleeping bag. Children must sleep in the bunkhouse during the week-long camps, and supervision is provided. The lodge, on the other hand, is quite lovely, a new building with "English Country" decor bedrooms and either private or shared baths. Children may stay with their parents in the lodge on weekend trips. All meals, prepared by Chef Al, a former restaurateur, are served family-style in the lodge dining room. Homemade soups are often served at lunch, while dinner typically features a simple but hearty rock cornish hen or chicken cacciatore. Special meals can be prepared for larger groups on request.

MINIMUM AGE: For week-long family riding camps, children must be at least eight years old.

RATES: Rates include all meals, riding lessons and trail riding, a hunt course, swimming pool and evening social activities. Adults, $399 per person, double occupancy in the lodge for one week. Children sleep in the bunkhouse for $325 each. Fall and spring weekend rates are $185 per person for adults in the lodge, $87 each for children; $145 per person in the bunkhouse, $80 each for children.

FOR MORE INFORMATION: Contact Honey Lane Farm, RFD 2–Box 127, Peterborough, N.H. 03458. Phone (603) 563-8078.

ON BICYCLE: TOURING AMERICA'S OPEN ROADS

What could make more sense? Your kids already spend half their lives on their bicycles, especially in the summer. Why not join them? Family bicycle touring is an excellent way to get some exercise and fresh air, get away from home, and to take a look at the countryside from a different perspective.

You may already know the joys of riding on the open road, through scenic villages and down country lanes. If you own a fairly new 10-speed or better bike, you also know how much bicycle technology has improved in the past 15 years. But if you have an old three-speed in the garage, or haven't ridden since you were a kid, you have a pleasant surprise in store. Modern multi-speed bikes are a pleasure to ride, as they make climbing hills much easier.

There are two ways to get into bicycle touring. If all the family members already own bikes, you can start by planning a short half-day trip somewhere in your area—on some quiet country roads, or through a pretty residential neighborhood you don't often visit, for instance. Then, when you're ready for an extended trip, you can either join a packaged tour or plan your own longer trip. Tips for planning your own tours are given on page 61 in the ON YOUR OWN section.

If you don't have your own bikes, another way to begin bike touring is to join a packaged tour put together by an established cycle touring company. Packaged tours vary widely in terms of what's provided, and what level of cycling ability is required. On packaged tours for novice bicyclists, you can ride across flat terrain or gently rolling hills, using 12-speed bikes provided by the tour operator, and sleep in luxurious accommodations at night. These tours are also usually van-supported, which means that you don't have to bear the burden of carrying your gear on your bike. A tour-operated van follows along the route, toting your luggage from one inn to the next, and sometimes delivering gourmet picnic lunches to pre-arranged locations during the day. This is in contrast to the tours put together for die-hard cyclists who ship their own bikes to the tour location, then ride for 35–60 miles each day, carrying all their clothing and camping gear on bike carriers so that they can camp out each night. The latter is an exhilarating vacation for people who are in top physical condition, but let's face it—most children, especially those under 13 or 14 years of age, wouldn't be able to keep up.

Another reason to choose a van-supported tour is that if for some reason you want to cut short your bicycling for the day—let's say your kids fall apart after the first six miles and the scheduled route is a 10-mile ride—the van driver will gladly pick you up and give you a lift to that night's lodging. Unless you've grossly overestimated your level of fitness or your kids' stamina, though, you probably won't need to call for a midday van pickup. Each tour offers a choice of shorter and longer routes so that you can tailor the length of each day's ride to your own family's ability. For instance, Day One of a tour might give you a choice of cycling for 7, 30, 46 or 54 miles. The first is the obvious choice for nonathletes, new cyclists and young children. On the other hand, if one family member is a real road warrior, he or she can choose the longer route, which usually branches off from the shorter one, to get a good workout.

If you don't own a bicycle or you don't want to bring one, you can rent an excellent adult touring bike or mountain bike from the tour operators for a moderate fee. If you do have a bike and wish to, you may ship it to the tour's starting point. In any case, you'll have to bring your kids' own bikes along because most tour operators don't rent children's bikes. Older kids who are at least 4'8" tall may be able to ride a rented adult bike with a 19" frame. Helmets are sometimes provided free of charge, sometimes available for rent. Bring your kids' helmets along, though, to insure good fit.

In general, bicycle touring works well for families with children ages eight or nine and up, or beginning when your children can ride their own bikes comfortably for an extended period of time. Teenagers do well on bike trips because the touring concept allows them the freedom to get away from mom and/or dad for chunks of time, while still participating in the family adventure.

A final few words to the wise: Most tours are led by two experienced group leaders who cycle with the group. Together with the van driver, they are knowledgeable about bike repairs and maintenance. The leaders also should be certified in CPR and first-aid. Nonetheless, in most ways, you are on your own. The leaders encourage people to cycle at their own pace, which means that a few top-notch cyclists will jump to the head of the pack, setting a grueling pace for themselves, while others dawdle along, enjoying the scenery or stopping to investigate some interesting landmark on the route. There may be miles between you and the leaders, or between you and the other cyclists in your group. You're expected to be able to read and follow the well-marked maps and route notes provided by the tour operator to get you to your destination.

Every now and then the group leaders and the support van will make a "sweep" of the route, but they don't actually accompany you every inch of the way. If you don't show up for lunch, they'll begin to worry. They'll call the inn to find out if you've left a distress message. If you're still missing at dinnertime, they'll call the police. But don't expect a personal escort on the trip. In assessing your family's readiness for bicycle touring, consider that in the worst of circumstances—if you get lost, or have an accident, for instance—you may have to rely on your own wits and resources until you can rejoin the group.

Later in this chapter, I've described a handful of tour operators selected for the outstanding quality of their tours and the wide variety of geographical selections. Send for their brochures and be dazzled by the photos and information about tours in Hawaii, Ireland or the Grand Canyon! For a more extensive list of tour operators, you can contact Bikecentennial, which is a nonprofit organization that promotes cycling (see page 64).

As the saying goes, once you've learned how to ride a bicycle, you never forget. Well, once you've taken an overnight bicycle tour, you've got something else you will never forget: memories.

GETTING IN SHAPE FOR A TOUR

Although many tours are designed for beginning riders, with short, flat routes and van lifts when necessary, you'll undoubtedly enjoy your bicycle tour more if you've had some bicycling experience before you go. To get into shape for a weekend tour, you and your family may want to start out by taking short rides of an hour, two hours, or half a day, depending on your level of fitness. Follow the guidelines in the ON YOUR OWN section beginning on page 61 for tips on taking self-guided tours of half a day or more. And, unless your bike has an odometer, measure your distance traveled by driving along your bike route, checking your car's odometer. That way you'll know how it feels to bike for 2 miles, 5 miles or 10 miles at a time.

Conditioning

If you're planning a week-long bicycle tour, it's a good idea to begin conditioning at least 30 days prior to the trip. Part of the conditioning is simply getting your heart and lungs into shape, so any aerobic activity is appropriate. Before beginning an exercise program, however, always check with your doctor, especially if you're over 30 or have a history of health problems. Once you have the go-ahead from your physician, try to exercise at least three times a week, engaging in some aerobic activity that will increase your pulse rate to about 65 percent of its maximum while exercising. (Your physician can provide you with a simple formula for determining what 65 percent of your maximum heart rate is.) Continue to exercise at this rate for at least 20 minutes to promote cardiovascular conditioning.

One indication of fitness is recovery time, that is, the time it takes your pulse to return to normal after exercising. Note your pulse before you begin to exercise, and then again when you stop. Wait two or three minutes after you've stopped and check your pulse rate again. If your pulse rate continues at the same rate as when you were exercising for more than four minutes after you've stopped, you are probably pushing yourself too hard. Back off a bit on your conditioning program until you've gradually built up some strength and stamina.

Here are some tour operators you should consider working with once your family's bodies are ready to roll:

VERMONT COUNTRY CYCLERS/ FOUR SEASONS CYCLING

Two well-established bicycle touring companies joined forces in 1989 and—under one management now—offer some of the best cycling packages for families. (In the interest of brevity, both tour operators will be referred to as "VCC" throughout this section, although certain tours originate from Four Seasons Cycling locations.)

Imagine hopping on a well-tuned 12-speed bike and setting out across the countryside at your own pace, cycling through California's Russian River country, or past the sandy beaches of Maryland's Chesapeake Bay, or through the gently rolling country lanes and covered bridges of Manchester, Vermont. At midday, you join a group of 20 other cyclists for a gourmet picnic lunch, then continue when you're ready, stopping perhaps to gaze at horses grazing near a 200-year-old maple tree. At day's end, you meet your tour group again at a charming, antique-filled country inn where you will be staying for the night. Dinner, magnificently prepared and served by candlelight, is topped off with an irresistible dessert. In the morning you burn off the extra calories of the previous night's indulgence when your bicycle tour begins again, this time off on another scenic route.

If that sounds ideal, then VCC bicycle tours are the perfect family adventure for you. What makes VCC tours great for families is the fact that the shorter tours are designed to accommodate varying levels of fitness and cycling experience in locations that are intrinsically appealing. The two-day weekend tours and three-day midweek tours, in particular, offer shorter routes with as few as seven miles of cycling per day, which would be most appropriate for younger children.

On all VCC trips, you spend each night in one of the area's finest country inns or resorts, dining on excellent food and enjoying the best accommodations available. Many of these tours are based in New England, an area known for its natural beauty and charming colonial villages. But there are also tours in other areas, including Washington, D.C.; Vail, Colorado; Florida; the North Carolina coast; and Pennsylvania Dutch country.

For families, VCC recommends selecting a tour that features a wide variety of recreational activities in addition to cycling so that your children won't get bored or antsy when the day's riding is over. For example, the Northeast Kingdom Explorer tour, centered in and around Craftsbury, Vermont, includes opportunities for sailing, tennis, swimming, an alpine slide ride and more.

The George Washington Country Explorer tour, which offers you the chance to see some of the monuments, museums and landmarks in Washington D.C. while on the tour, is also great for families. An added advantage of the Washington Tour is that all of the routes used are bona fide bicycle paths—which means that your children will not have to negotiate traffic. For many miles, the bike paths run parallel to a system of canals and locks stretching all the way into Cumberland, Maryland. Other tours particularly well-suited to families are the Moose Mountain weekend, the Manchester Center weekend, the Pennsylvania Dutch tours, the Three Mountain Backroad Explorer trip, and for older children the week-long Maine Coast Windjammer tour which combines sailing and bicycling.

MINIMUM AGE: eight years old.

RATES: Sample price for a typical two-day weekend tour, including inn lodging with private bath, two meals each day (breakfast and dinner), tour leaders, maps and written directions, and support van: $279 per person, double occupancy for adults; children 8 to 12 receive a 25 percent discount when sharing a room with parents. Bicycle rental for the weekend is an additional $50 per bike. A typical five-day Explorer trip with the same meals, lodging, and amenities costs $679 per person, double occupancy; bike rentals are $79 for five days; children receive the same 25 percent discount when sharing their parents' room. Gourmet picnic lunches, available on the week-long trips only, are $25 per week, per person.

FOR MORE INFORMATION: Contact Vermont Country Cyclers, P.O. Box 145, Waterbury Center, Vt. 05677. Phone (802) 244-8751.

BACKROADS BICYCLE TOURING, INC.

This first-rate tour operator has excellent credentials among cycling enthusiasts and a multitude of tour locations to appeal to nearly any family. Elegant inn tours in California, Virginia, Louisiana, Yellowstone Park, Maine and Vermont (to name just a few) offer spectacular scenery and superb accommodations and dining.

There are also camping tours which offer the same wonderful scenery at a lower price. But this is camping the easy way, as Backroads provides all the equipment and the staff transports the gear by van or trailer from one campsite to the next. Meals are even prepared for you; all you do is set up your own tent (after a little instruction from the tour guides). These camping/cycling tours are a great way for adventurous families to try out two new sports in one fantastic, relaxed vacation.

Backroads also arranges international tours which originate in France, Ireland, Italy, China and even Bali! Note, though, that most of these tours are designed for intermediate and advanced riders.

MINIMUM AGE: Flexible and variable, depending on the trip. Backroads recommends that children be at least six years old.

RATES: Sample price for a typical two-day weekend inn tour, including all meals and snacks, lodging, tour leaders, maps, helmets and van support: $368 per adult, double occupancy. Discounts for children sharing a room with adults are 50 percent for children 6 and under; 25 percent for ages 7–12; 10 percent for ages 13–16. The same camping/cycling weekend trip will cost $179 per adult, double occupancy, with the same discounts for children. Bicycle rentals and trip cancellation insurance are available for an additional fee.

FOR MORE INFORMATION: Contact Backroads Bicycle Touring, 1516 5th Street, Berkeley, Calif. 94710. Phone (800) 533-2573; in Calif. (415) 527-1555.

COUNTRY CYCLING TOURS

Delightful weekend inn tours and romantic week-long explorations are the specialty of this East Coast tour operator. Among the more unusual offerings is the New England Island-Hopping Vacation, which takes you from Martha's Vineyard to Nantucket to Newport for five days of enjoyable island cycling with dramatic ocean views.

Country Cycling Tours also organizes some more exotic tours. There are real-life Asian jungle adventures, including a Thailand bicycle journey and a 19-day tour of China by cycle and rail. Other international tours include the Loire Valley in France, Barbados, England, Ireland and more.

At the other end of the spectrum there are one-day outings in the New York City area, for example. For a very reasonable fee (between $20 and $40 per person) you can join a group of cyclists who spend the day exploring the New York wine country, or the south shore of Long Island or the pastoral farmlands of Dutchess County, New York.

MINIMUM AGE: None, although the tour operator will make recommendations for specific tours.

RATES: Typical price for a three-day bicycling weekend, including lodging, most meals, maps, van support and tour guides: $399 per adult, double occupancy. Bicycle rental is $57 per person for the weekend. Discounts are available for children under 12, and for families of 4 or more.

FOR MORE INFORMATION: Contact Country Cycling Tours, 140 W. 83rd Street, New York, N.Y. 10024. Phone (212) 874-5151.

MICHIGAN BICYCLE TOURING

Although this tour operator is smaller and more regionally focused than the others mentioned above, it is just as committed to providing a fun, safe, relaxing and first-class cycling experience with all the amenities that the larger tours afford. All tours originate in Michigan, a state with magnificent waterfalls, pristine sandy beaches and panoramic shorelines. Particularly suitable for families is the tour on Mackinac Island—a cyclist's paradise because no automobiles are allowed on the island! Food supplies, people, and even the garbage on the island are all transported by horse-drawn vehicles—or by bike! The island's wilderness shoreline, the elegant Grand Hotel perched overlooking Lake Huron, and the quaint island village offers something for everyone's vacation pleasure.

Other family-oriented vacations include the pedal-and-paddle trips in which you cycle around the shoreline of Crystal Lake, and then canoe on one of the gently flowing rivers of Michigan, watching for mute swans and great blue herons. Catered picnics are provided for some trips.

MINIMUM AGE: None. Michigan Bicycle Touring requires the use of a cart rather than a child seat for transporting nonbiking children. These carts, which attach securely to most adult bicycles and are able to pull two small children, are available for $20 per day.

RATES: All tour prices are double occupancy and include lodging, meals, gratuities, tour leaders, maps, written directions, canoe rentals, ferry trips and luggage transportation where applicable. The two-day Mackinac Island trip costs $249 per adult. Discounts for children under 3 are 75 percent of the tour price; 50 percent for ages 3–6; 25 percent for ages 7–12; and 15 percent for ages 13–16. Bicycle rental rates range from $39 for two days to $89 for five days. Eighteen-speed tandems are also available at higher rates.

FOR MORE INFORMATION: Contact Michigan Bicycle Touring, 3512 Red School Road, Kingsley, Mich. 49649. Phone (616) 263-5885.

BICYCLE TOURING ON YOUR OWN

The key to bicycle touring on your own is to start with a one-day ride in the country or a half-day ride around town. If you or your kids bail out after the first three miles, you won't be far from home.

To begin with, you'll need to plan a route. Make it a short trip that covers mostly flat or gently rolling terrain in low traffic areas, preferably in a loop that circles around and returns you to your car. Of course it's possible to ride "out and back"; i.e., to travel a certain number of miles out along a road and then double back to the starting point. But who wants to bike the same route twice in one day? It's more fun to just keep going for miles and miles, seeing new sights all the way. Your sense of adventure will increase and your children will have more fun if you ride along a loop route.

There are a few basic items you need to take along on a bike tour, even a short one. The most important thing is water. Cycling—and the sweating that goes with it—can quickly deplete your body of fluids, which need to be replaced. Each cyclist should have his or her own water bottle, mounted in a cage on the bike frame. Take a few sips every 15–20 minutes, more often in very hot weather. This is essential and can't be stressed enough, because novice cyclists and kids often find themselves having such a great time that they don't realize that their bodies are becoming dehydrated. So make a rule that everyone stops for a "group slurp" at least three times an hour.

Another vitally important item for bike touring is a helmet. If you wear one, then your kids will be more willing to wear their helmets, too. Helmets are the single most important safety precaution you can take when cycling. If you doubt the need for a helmet, just remember: a broken bone will mend but a head injury may not.

Other high-priority gear for a half-day or all-day bike tour includes: map, bike tool kit, tire patch kit, tire pump, compass, bike lock, rain poncho, small first-aid kit and money (including change for telephone calls). You might also want sun block, sunglasses, insect repellent, a picnic lunch and some plastic bags for trash, wet clothing, etc.

You can carry most of your gear in a backpack, a handlebar bag, or in a special "saddlebag" called a pannier. Panniers are designed to attach to a bike carrier mounted over your rear wheel. For carrying small things like money and keys, a "fanny pack" worn around your waist works well.

As for cycling clothes, you can really wear anything on a short trip, as long as you're comfortable. For a longer trip, you might want to try the skin-tight cycling shorts, which help prevent chafing and "saddle burn." The best shorts have a seamless crotch lined with cotton or chamois. Closely fitting jerseys are also a good idea, since they reduce wind resistance. On your feet, you'll need running shoes or tennis shoes to help grip the pedals and distribute the pressure across the sole of your foot.

Once you've made it through your first bicycle tour, you may feel adventurous enough to want to plan your own overnight trip. Depending on where you plan to sleep, you may need to carry a lot of equipment on your bike (tents, cooking gear, and sleeping bags), or you can simply throw in a toothbrush and a change of clothes. In any event, the first rule of the road is: Travel light. Don't take anything you won't absolutely need, and try to keep your load to about 30 pounds maximum for teenagers and adults, 15 pounds maximum for children under 14. Take snacks and plenty of water, but don't take a lot of food. Most cycling campers buy food one day at a time, on the road, rather than add anything more to their load.

Biking maps which describe or illustrate the hills on each route and indicate special bike paths along the way are crucial for planning a do-it-yourself tour. You can buy these maps from various biking organizations, including Bikecentennial (see page 64.) You may also be able to get biking maps free from your own state's Department of Transportation, Department of Tourism or the Department of Parks and Recreation.

The big question about an on-your-own overnight bike tour is where should you sleep at night. The choices are many. You can plan a country inn trip, in which you stay at an inn or bed-and-breakfast, bike in the surrounding countryside every day and return to the same inn each night. This is a great plan for first-time, do-it-yourself weekend tours. The scenery, meals and accommodations would be similar to those in the packaged tours described earlier in this chapter, but you would have no tour leaders or support van for emergencies. Note, though, the fact that many country inns do not accept children under the age of 12 or 13, so you may have to do some research to find the right combination of routes, scenery, easy biking terrain and inn accommodations.

Another option is to camp out. This is a much more complicated endeavor, recommended only to families who have already done some camping on their own. Camping, after all, puts you in a fairly vulnerable position: Family against Nature, and all that. Most campers take comfort in the knowledge that if their own resources fail, they can quickly run back to the car and drive to civilization. On a biking tour, you don't have that safety net, so you're twice as vulnerable. If you're eager to try biking and camping, however, pick up a copy of *The Complete Book of Bicycling* by Eugene A. Sloane (Simon and Schuster). This is one of the best books about cycling, with lots of material about what to pack, how to select a tent just for bicycle camping and so forth.

Perhaps the most economical overnight tour option is to sleep at a youth hostel. This is sort of a compromise between camping and staying in a motel or inn. American Youth Hostels, with more than 200 locations all over the United States, offer no-frills, dormitory-style rooms at a very low price, often as little as $5 per night! You must bring your own food, towels and a special sleeping sack, which can easily be packed into a pannier. It's rustic, but it's also a very sociable kind of adventure, and great for families on a tight budget.

If you arrive without a reservation, you will be assigned to a room with other people of the same gender. For this reason, certain minimum age limits apply. Children traveling and rooming with an adult of the same sex must be at least five years old. Children traveling with an adult of the opposite sex must be at least 10 years old, since the child will be separated from the adult at night. Clearly the best course is to make a reservation in advance, requesting a family bedroom, so that you can all stay together.

For information about membership, which is open to people of all ages, write to American Youth Hostels, Inc., P.O. Box 37613, Washington, D.C. 20013. Phone (202) 783-6161.

ANOTHER RESOURCE

Bikecentennial is a nonprofit organization that promotes cycling and sponsors its own bicycle tours. Bikecentennial's tours are *not* for families, but the organization does publish a great resource guide to cycling, *The Cyclists' Yellow Pages*. This book contains information about dozens of tour operators, some of whom gear tours to novices and families. Bikecentennial members can also purchase bicycle route maps for all parts of the United States. These maps are invaluable for planning your own trips, because they contain vital information about the terrain. Bikecentennial's own tour catalog contains good information about such matters as how to choose a bike, how to get into shape for a tour and how to pack your bike for airline travel.

FOR MORE INFORMATION: Contact Bikecentennial, P.O. Box 8308, Missoula, Mont. 59807. Phone (406) 721-1776.

ON SKIS: DOWNHILL AND CROSS-COUNTRY

Broken bones . . . expensive equipment . . . intimidating crowds of super-athletes . . . a singles social scene . . . fear . . . posh and pricey accommodations . . . chic clothes . . . more broken bones . . .

If you have stayed away from downhill skiing for any or all of these reasons, join the club. Hundreds of families are intrigued by the notion of a skiing adventure, but never get past the daydreaming stage. They are

afraid—of being embarrassed, or injured or both. And who can blame them? After all, there are few sources of information aimed at the nonskier, and practically none that you feel you can trust. Perhaps you've asked a good friend or neighbor about downhill skiing, and he has responded with wild enthusiasm, "Sure! You'll love it! It's great! You can take lessons and there are small slopes for beginners. Give it a try!" But if you're like many nonskiers, you only half believe the advice of those who have already mastered the sport. They're obviously more coordinated and more athletic than you are, and besides—they already love it. What if you spend all that money—and you don't love it?

The truth is that if you're at all interested in trying a skiing adventure, you probably *will* love it. Many of the physical hazards of downhill skiing—the broken bones, sprained ankles and such—have been reduced in recent years thanks to technological advances in ski equipment and better grooming of ski trails. The expense of downhill skiing is not prohibitive if you rent equipment, which makes sense for the first time out. And the crowds of super-athletes can be avoided if you choose the ski area carefully. Novices don't belong on the monster slopes anyway.

So the real question becomes: Are you willing to try a sport that your children are likely to learn more quickly than you? It can be mildly humiliating, but well worth it. Most families find that learning to ski together creates fantastic memories ("I'll never forget how funny Dad looked when he fell face-first into that pile of snow!") and generates a great feeling of closeness. By the end of a skiing trip, you've shared in the trials and tribulations of freezing cold weather, you've waited in lift lines together and you've felt some of the same frustrations. In short, it's a bonding experience that can't be beat.

This section, then, is for people who have never tried downhill skiing before, or for families who want the best in beginner ski experiences, even if one family member is an old pro on the slopes. If you're not even remotely interested in downhill skiing, skip to the end of this chapter and plow into the section on cross-country skiing. Cross-country, as you may know, is an excellent fitness exercise, much less expensive than downhill, and generally regarded as one of the easiest (and most gratifying) winter sports to learn.

ABOUT KIDS ON SKIS

At what age can children learn to ski? Some ski fanatics will tell you that they put their children on skis as soon as they learned to walk. But the nationally organized program of ski lessons for children, called SKIwee, generally begins offering lessons to children at age four. SKIwee programs are available at many ski resort areas; the program usually offers all-day skiing and lessons for kids in various age groups. If you have a large family, with several ski-aged children and an infant or toddler, you can still go on a family skiing adventure by selecting a resort area that has daycare facilities for very young children.

GETTING READY

There are a few things you'll want to consider before throwing your clothes into a suitcase and dashing off to the slopes. The first is cold-weather clothing: What should you take and how should you dress for the slopes? The second is conditioning. In order to get the most out of your first skiing experience—and lower your chances of injury—you should engage in some pre-ski adventure fitness training. Many injuries are preventable, especially the most common ones: sprained ankles and torn ligaments.

Clothing

Let's talk about clothing first. If you've never been skiing, you may not be adequately prepared for just how cold it can be on a mountain, with the wind blowing and the sun hiding. Add to that the fact that you may be standing in long lines for the ski lifts, then sitting still as you ride the unenclosed chairs up, up, up into the wind for 10 minutes or more. In other words, you need to dress more warmly than you would for an average romp in the snow in your local park or own backyard. The following items are essential:

▶ Long underwear, preferably made of a material that wicks away your perspiration. Silk is great, but expensive. Polypropylene is another choice.

▶ Ski jacket or parka. The nylon shell is usually waterproof, making a ski parka preferable to a wool jacket.

▶ Quilted ski pants which fit over your ski boots are ideal for regular (cold) ski conditions. As an alternative, you and your children can wear jeans and nylon windbreaker pants. Having the nylon pants on over the jeans will keep you dry when you fall in the snow. The slim, stretch ski pants which are tapered to fit inside your boots are fine for warmer ski-weather situations.

▶ A thin sock, layered with a medium-thick wool sock is your best bet. Wear *your* ski socks when being fitted for ski boots.

▶ Thin turtleneck shirts and sweaters, and thicker crew neck sweaters, also for layering. Turtlenecks are important because they do the work of scarves, which can be a safety hazard—they can get caught in the lift equipment or tangled in your poles.

▶ Warm, wool knitted (or down or fur) hat or a headband that can cover the ears.

▶ Gloves or mittens, preferably good quality ski gloves. Considering how much contact a new skier is likely to have with the snow, it's worth it to invest in good gloves or mittens. Some of them are even made with Gore-tex, which *really* keeps your hands dry and warm.

▶ Ski goggles or sunglasses are a must as the snow can be blinding.

▶ Wrist bands (the stretchy terrycloth ones worn by joggers). If your jacket or gloves don't feature good bands (and they *really* should), wearing wrist bands is a great way to keep snow from getting in your gloves every time you fall down. Wear them just inside your gloves so that they more or less plug up the opening.

As for ski boots, opinions are divided on whether you should buy them before your trip, or wait to see whether you really like the sport. If you're like most adults, you'll probably choose to rent boots the first time you go skiing, since buying ski boots can be very expensive. Then, if you fall in love with skiing, boots will be your first investment. You might even decide to buy your boots at a ski shop while you're on vacation. But remember that it's usually more expensive to buy equipment at the resort than it is to buy it at home.

On the other hand, if you've ever rented ice skates, you know it's not fun to be in someone else's shoes. So if money is no object, by all means buy the boots before you go.

For children whose feet are still growing, you'll probably want to stick with rental boots until your kids are in their late teens—or until they become certified ski maniacs.

Whether you rent or buy, you'll be doing business in a ski shop. At most ski areas, there are always several in town and one near the base of the mountain. The town shops will be less expensive than the slopeside ski shops, but you'll have to tote your rented skis, poles and boots to and from the mountain on or in your car. Since the skis will be wet on the way back, transporting them inside the car isn't such a good idea—assuming they even fit! For this reason, you'll probably want to rent your equipment at the slope if you're driving your own car. If you're driving a rented car, on the other hand, it may be equipped with a roof rack for skis; they're widely available at car rental outlets in ski resort areas. If you want to save money by renting ski equipment at a town ski shop, be sure to rent a car with a roof rack, too. Clip-on roof racks are widely available at ski/sports shops, are inexpensive and easy to install.

Conditioning

Basically, skiing requires flexibility, quick reflexes and some leg muscle tone rather than cardiovascular conditioning. If you or your kids are swimmers, for instance, you may still need to begin a special conditioning program in order to develop your skiing muscles. Walking, stretching, stair climbing and bent-knee sit-ups are all good exercises to start with. But don't stop there. Pick up a book on skiing and check out the chapters on conditioning. Or join an exercise group at your local YMCA or health club. Your goal is to develop enough muscle tone so that your legs won't tire on the first day of your vacation; and, even more important, to stretch the muscles and ligaments in your legs and back, so that, in a fall, they can withstand some strain without tearing. Start about a month before you plan to take your first ski trip, and gradually increase your exercise program to build strength.

Be sure to include your kids in the conditioning program, too. Even if they're in great shape—even if, like most kids, they have great reflexes and remarkably flexible joints—it's still a good idea to get them working on the specific muscles that are used in skiing. It's a small investment of time that will pay off handsomely on your vacation.

A word of advice: take lessons. Most experts agree that ski lessons—even brush-up lessons for intermediate and advanced skiers—are invaluable in preventing injuries and increasing your enjoyment of the sport. If you've never skied, you're undoubtedly planning to take an introductory lesson or two. Better yet, plan to take a whole week of lessons. Most people can pretty much nail down the basics in a week. Group lessons are fine for beginners, both kids and adults. But once you and/or your children have mastered the basics, you may find that it's worthwhile to schedule private lessons. Also remember that you and your children may progress at different rates. Soon, you'll find that you're in one class and they're in another. (They may be way ahead of you!) Be sure to book ski lessons at the same time you make reservations for lodging.

RATES: The typical cost for one-day rental of downhill ski equipment is $18 for adults, $12 for children, with discounts for multiday rentals widely available. Lift tickets at larger resorts cost, on average, about $36 per day for adults and $19 per day for children. Certain exceptional value packages, however, can present big savings for families: For instance, when an adult skis during the week for five days at Stowe,

Vermont, the lift ticket costs $110 and children ski free. Typical rates for ski lessons: $22 per adult in a two-hour group lesson; $42 per hour for a private lesson, with an additional person charged $15. Children's programs, which include ski lessons and lunch but not equipment rentals, cost about $36 per day, $160 for five days. Daycare for infants and toddlers can be costly, nearly as much as the skiing itself.

WHERE TO SKI: DOWNHILL

While Aspen, Sun Valley and Jackson Hole may be the resort areas that immediately leap to mind when you think of skiing, you won't want to begin your family's first skiing adventure at any one of those. Those famous ski resorts and places such as Killington or Stowe, Vermont, are popular for a reason: They offer excellent skiing challenges for people who have already mastered smaller mountains and are ready for bigger thrills. That is not necessarily you. On the other hand, just because you and your kids are beginners doesn't mean that you have to head for the smallest, most out-of-the-way ski area. Rather, you'll very likely be happiest at a well-known and well-equipped ski resort, where the quality of the ski lessons is superior and the ski trails are well maintained.

For a weekend outing, choose a ski destination relatively close to your home. Although the Western mountains are considerably higher than their Eastern counterparts they boast many manageable slopes for beginners. No need to fly from San Francisco to Montreal, Vermont or Maine just to avoid the Rocky Mountains. Lots of people have learned to ski in Colorado, and you can, too.

Some of the best locations for beginner skiing are listed on the following pages, arranged by geographical region. In most ski resort areas, a visitor's bureau or lodging bureau acts as a clearinghouse for information about accommodations. All you need do is write or phone that agency to obtain a mountain of information, including brochures from various inns, resorts, motels and such. Some bureaus will make reservations for you as well.

When requesting information about a ski resort, don't forget to ask about the specific features of interest to you. For instance:

▶ What percentage of the ski trails are designated as beginner or "easy" trails?

▶ Is snowmaking equipment used? If so, on how much of the terrain, and how often are the trails groomed? (Even though you're not a hotshot yet, you'll want to ski on well-covered slopes, not patches of dirt and grass! And you'll find it easier to descend a slope that has been recently groomed, since grooming removes those tricky bumps called "moguls.")

▶ Is there free skiing and/or free lodging for children? Is there a good children's program? For what ages is the program and what does it include? Some ski resorts offer childcare programs for infants to three-year-olds. Others only offer ski lessons and supervised fun and games for toddlers and up.

▶ Are there cross-country skiing trails?

▶ Are special beginner packages available, including ski rental, lessons and lift tickets?

▶ Which days of the week are least crowded? How long is the average waiting time for the ski lifts? Is there a limited lift ticket policy, which limits the number of people who can ski that day? If so, how can you get lift tickets in advance?

And, of course, you should get all the details about costs. When figuring the cost of a ski adventure vacation, remember to factor in transportation to the resort area, meals and lodging, ski rentals (boots, bindings, poles and skis), ski lessons and lift tickets. (Lift tickets, in case you were wondering, are the manner in which ski resorts charge you for use of the mountain. In other words, you don't have to pay to ski down the mountain—just to go up it!)

Following is a small selection of ski resorts ideal for first-time family skiing. At each location, you'll be able to find a variety of accommodations— everything from ski lodges to boarding houses to rental condos to resort hotels—in a wide range of prices. When contacting the bureaus of lodging and tourism, ask for recommendations in your specific price range so you can narrow the choices. But, if possible, don't make your choice on the basis of price alone. The après-ski atmosphere you'll find in many lodges is a good part of the fun!

For more information, you may also want to consult *Fodor's Skiing in North America* (Random House), available in bookstores and libraries.

IN THE EAST

BELLEAYRE MOUNTAIN SKI CENTER
Highmount, New York

Just a three-hour drive from New York City, Belleayre Mountain offers a relaxed, family atmosphere coupled with reasonably priced lift tickets and a special beginners' area on the lower part of the mountain. The slopes and nearby lodgings are less crowded than many other ski resorts in New York, and much less crowded than the big-name Vermont resorts. For information about a variety of inns, lodges and motels in the area, contact the Belleayre Mountain Lodging Bureau, Box 313, Highmount, N.Y. 12441. Phone (800) 431-6021; inside New York, (800) 257-7017.

SKI WINDHAM
Windham, New York
Formerly a private club, Ski Windham is now a quality public facility with well-groomed trails (which mean fewer bumps for beginners!) and snowmaking on almost 100 percent of the terrain. Beginners can ski a 2¼ mile trail which starts at the top of the mountain and provides great views—a welcome change from the "bunny" slopes found at most ski areas. Skiing is free to children 12 and under. Ski Windham is located about 150 miles from New York City. For a 44-page brochure featuring information about accommodations and other tourist activities in the area, contact the Greene County Tourism Department, Box 527, Catskill, N.Y. 12414. Phone (518) 943-3223.

MOUNT SNOW SKI RESORT
Mount Snow, Vermont
Vermont is skiing territory, plain and simple. If you're looking for an Eastern family adventure in which you not only learn to ski but also get to soak up some of the glamour and excitement associated with a ski resort atmosphere, then you'll want to head for Vermont sooner or later. Later perhaps, you will want to choose Killington which has the longest runs and steepest trails available in the East. But on your first outing, you'll be more at ease, and find just as much excitement, at a medium-sized resort like Mount Snow. Seventy-seven trails of all levels of difficulty blanket the mountain, attracting novice, intermediate and experts skiers alike. The "easy" trails begin at the top of the mountain, which is often sunny—an added bonus. And when you're finished skiing, your children will love the sleigh rides offered by several of the inns in the nearby town of Wilmington. Mount Snow is 30 miles west of Brattleboro, about 125 miles from Boston. For more information contact Mount Snow Vacation Services, Mount Snow, Vt. 05356. Phone (802) 464-8501.

CAMELBACK SKI AREA
Tannersville, Pennsylvania
With nearly half the terrain on Camelback rated in the "easiest" category, this is known as a beginner's paradise. Snowmaking is used on all the trails,

insuring good coverage. The mountain is not large—only 800 vertical feet—so the most competitive skiers are likely to go elsewhere, leaving you and your family to flail around in privacy and peace. There are many lodge rooms right on the mountain. Camelback is about 90 miles from both New York City and Philadelphia. For information about slopeside accommodations, contact Camelback Ski Area, Box 168, Tannersville, Pa. 18372. Phone (717) 629-1661. Additional information is available from the Pocono Mountain Vacation Bureau, 1040 Main St., Stroudsberg, Pa. 18360. Phone (717) 421-5791.

IN THE MIDWEST

CRYSTAL MOUNTAIN
Thompsonville, Michigan

The Midwest is a great place to learn to ski, since it's not what ski or travel buffs call a "ski destination," in other words experienced skiers rarely go out of their way to ski these slopes. Why not? Because the mountains simply aren't big enough to present many thrills and chills for the seasoned skier. A few Michigan ski resorts offer expert trails, and so does Crystal Mountain. But with only 375 vertical feet, this mountain looks like a molehill next to Aspen, Vail and Beaver Creek, which have 3000 vertical feet each.

Because it offers heavy discounts and freebies to beginning skiers and children, Crystal Mountain is an ideal choice for a first-time family adventure in skiing. An added attraction is the cross-country skiing which is available here. Crystal Mountain is about 15 miles from the airport in Traverse City, which has commuter line connections to airports in Chicago and Detroit.

For information about accommodations available in the Crystal Mountain area, contact Michigan RSVP, 8727 Palaestrum, Williamsburg, Mich. 49684. Phone (616) 267-5772.

IN THE WEST

STEAMBOAT SPRINGS
Steamboat Springs, Colorado

It's remote, that's for sure. And it's western, that's sure as shootin', too. Steamboat Springs, Colorado, deep in the heart of dude ranch country, is crawling with cowboys, coyotes and real honest-to-goodness hot springs bubbling right up out of the ground every season of the year. But that's not what brings skiers here by the carload in winter. It's the certified 3,600-foot vertical rise, the ton of snow and the change of pace from fancier (and pricier) ski resorts elsewhere in Colorado that attracts the serious skier and family to Steamboat.

The mountain itself is called Mt. Werner. It offers ski trails for every level of ability, including beginners, and a bonus for families: Kids ski free on visits of five days or more. Many motels and lodges offer free accommodations for children, too. There are other regional adventure opportunities as well, including dog sledding, snowmobiling, sleigh riding, ice fishing, skating and even hot air ballooning! When you've done it all, you can cool your heels—or, rather, warm them—in the natural hot mineral waters which feed the public pool in town.

Steamboat Springs is located about 150 miles northwest of Denver. For information and reservations, write to the Chamber Resort Association, Box 774408, Steamboat Springs, Colo. 80477. Phone (303) 879-0740.

WINTER PARK
Winter Park, Colorado

An easy 65-mile drive from Denver, excellent skiing for every level of ability, a wide selection of restaurants, including many which cater to the finicky tastes of children, and a distinct area set aside for beginning skiers make this ski resort a good choice for family fun. Only about 10 percent of the trails are serviced by snowmaking equipment—but that's okay, because Mother Nature usually takes care of this mountain. If you live in the area and are planning a spur-of-the-moment trip, check the snow report by phoning (303) 666-4502. Mary Jane, a ski area tailored to more advanced skiers, is nearby.

For information about lodging contact Winter Park Central Reservations, Box 36, Winter Park, Colo. 80482. Phone (800) 453-2525 or (303) 726-5587.

COPPER MOUNTAIN
Copper Mountain, Colorado

Talk to some die-hard ski bums and you'll undoubtedly hear about Copper Mountain. Set in an old mining town, as many of Colorado's ski resorts are, Copper Mountain offers a quaint combination of western flavor and luxurious resort atmosphere, and is nestled at the base of a ski slope with a 2,760-foot vertical rise. (The entire mountain is more than 11,000 feet high!) As with other Colorado locations, snowmaking is possible, though not generally required. Still, it's nice to have, especially when the weather turns your premium powder (the good kind of snow) into corn (the bad kind).

For families who want to brush elbows with top-notch skiers without buying the whole glitz-and-glamour package that comes with skiing at the upper-echelon resorts, Copper Mountain is a good choice. There's even a Club Med here, if you like your adventures packaged and paid for in one fell swoop. Copper Mountain is about 75 miles outside of Denver.

For more information contact Copper Mountain Lodging Services, Box 3001, Copper Mountain, Colo. 80443. Phone (800) 458-8386.

SUN VALLEY
Sun Valley, Idaho

Long known as the glamourous ski destination of the rich and famous, Sun Valley has a lot to offer a family of beginning skiers as well. For one thing, the town is cozy and compact—you can walk just about everywhere. For another, Dollar Mountain, with its perfectly groomed trails, is ideal for beginners. For more advanced skiers, there is Mt. Baldy. And best of all there is the sun itself, from whence the name comes. In fact, Sun Valley afficionados claim that the sun is so gloriously warm on the mountain that skiing here beats a beach vacation any time of year.

For more information contact Sun Valley Company, Sun Valley, Idaho 83353. From anywhere outside Idaho, phone (800) 635-8261. From within Idaho, phone (800) 632-4104.

HEAVENLY VALLEY
Stateline, Nevada

Literally just a stone's throw from the California state line, this ski resort is an excellent choice for beginners who want to find out what it feels like to ski from the top of an awesome geographical landmark. The beginner runs are at the summit, where the sun almost always shines, and they cover about 25 percent of the skiable terrain. Below the mountain is Lake Tahoe, icy cold any time of year and in a category all its own when it comes to sheer beauty.

There's only one drawback to Heavenly Valley, and it's a big one. The resort is tremendously busy, ranking as the third most popular ski resort in America, according to Rand McNally's *Vacation Places Rated.* That translates to more than 780,000 skier visits per year. To accommodate those crowds, the resort has super-efficient lift facilities able to cover an astounding 23 million vertical feet per hour! (That's the distance covered by each lift per hour multiplied by the number of lifts.)

Consequently, Heavenly Valley may not be the place for any but the most adventurous family. If you're tempted, there are some strategies to help you deal with the crowds. First of all, plan your trip to begin on a weekday rather than the weekend, as weekdays are less crowded. Secondly, consider a geographical maneuver. The resort actually spans both California and Nevada, with most tourist/skiers coming from the California side. So if you want to beat the crowds, try the Nevada accommodations. They'll be less expensive, although you won't be able to take your children into any of the casinos—a fact that will limit your dining opportunities.

Heavenly Valley is about 175 miles east of San Francisco. For information or reservations, phone Heavenly Valley Central Reservations at (800) 2-HEAVEN or (702) 588-4584.

CROSS-COUNTRY SKIING

There you are, out in the middle of a winter wonderland, surrounded by evergreens, with the white snow at your feet and a palpable stillness in the air. There are no footprints in sight—only the tracks of the animals who live in these woods you are so quietly exploring. It's cold outside, but you aren't really aware of it because the kick-glide, kick-glide activity you're engaged in is keeping you warm. Everywhere you look, you find the beauty of unspoiled nature.

That's what it's like to go cross-country skiing. It's a winter sport that's practically tailor-made for families, because it's easy enough for almost any age child to do and it's definitely more fun in a group.

Cross-country skiing, also called Nordic skiing and ski touring—and X-C for short—has been around for many, many years, having originated not as a sport but as a practical means of getting around in Scandinavia. It has at least half a dozen advantages over downhill skiing. For one thing, you can ski cross-country anywhere there's snow. You don't need to travel to a ski resort area; in fact, if you live in a northern climate, you can often do it within a few miles of your own front door. The equipment is less expensive than downhill skiing, the surroundings are less crowded and just as beautiful, the chance of injury is practically nil and best of all, you can master cross-country skiing with only one or two short lessons. In fact, in a pinch, you can even teach yourself to cross-country ski, with the aid of a well-written book like *Cross-Country Skiing For the Fun of It* by Margaret Bennett (Dodd, Mead and Company).

Your best bet, however, first time out, is to pack your family into the car and head for the nearest ski touring center. There you'll be able to rent X-C skis, boots and poles (all of the equipment used for cross-country is different from downhill equipment, so don't try to mix and match). At the ski touring center, you and your children can take a one-hour lesson together, which should be sufficient to get all of you going. There will be X-C beginner trails, well-marked, and maps of the trails will be available. You'll have to pay a fee to use the trails, but compared with the costs of downhill, the fees are very reasonable at an average of $4–$12 per person. Even at an expensive resort area such as Mohonk in upstate New York, the cost for day guests using the X-C trails is only $7 for adults and $5 for children.

If you find you like cross-country, you'll probably want to buy your own equipment and take another lesson or two. And that's about all there is to it. Oh, sure, you can obsess on this sport, just like any other. You could get into racing, or cross-country mountaineering. But for most people, cross-country is on a par with riding a bike: It takes a few hours or days to master the technique, and after that, you just have fun!

Getting Ready

Dressing for cross-country skiing is different from dressing for downhill skiing, mainly because in X-C, you spend more of your time in motion and have to expend more (warming) energy. Consequently, you need to dress in layers. You should bring a backpack containing extra layers you can add, in case the weather is colder than you anticipated. More often, however, you'll find yourself peeling off layers as your body furnace gets cranked up, at which point you'll *really* be glad you have a place to put the clothing you've stripped off. Beginners tend to tire quickly because they often over-dress. So bring a backpack and plan for all eventualities—cold, hot and everything in between.

Here's what your layers should consist of: long underwear made of wool or polypropylene (which wicks away moisture caused by perspiration), wool pants, wool shirt, wool hat, windbreaker, scarf (worn tucked inside) and insulated gloves or mittens.

In your backpack, bring an extra sweater and—*very important*—bring water! As with bicycling, running and other aerobic sports, you'll be burning a lot of calories and sweating away your fluids. So don't even think of setting out for a morning on the cross-country trails without enough water for the whole family. You'll also need some food for snacks: trail mix, fruit and bagels are good energy boosters.

Equipment

As for skiing equipment, plan to rent, rather than buy, your first time out. Be sure to ask for waxless skis. These are much easier for beginners to use, as there is less muss and fuss. The other type—skis that require wax—require a great deal more expertise to use because there are dozens of kinds of wax, each one suited to certain snow conditions. When properly waxed, these X-C skis are more efficient. But it takes time to learn how to judge the conditions and apply the right kind of wax. If and when you decide to buy X-C equipment, then you may want to learn about wooden or waxable skis. Do a little research first to find out about the pros and cons of each kind.

About Kids and Cross-Country Skiing

Children can cross-country ski, as soon as they can walk and run with confidence. In Scandinavia, where X-C isn't so much a sport as a way of life, two- and three-year-olds ski cross-country regularly. In fact, if your children are very young, their stamina may out-distance yours. Novice skiers, whether children or adults, can generally endure a 1½-hour outing before tiring. The only drawback to taking very young children on a cross-country trek is that they may be more enchanted with the snow than anything else. They may spend all of their time playing and rolling around in the white stuff, while you're nagging them to keep moving! To avoid that kind of frustration, plan your X-C outing for an afternoon, following a morning romp in the snow for your little ones.

Ski Touring Centers and Resorts

Most wide open spaces with snowfall are ideal cross- country skiing territory. So it's not surprising that many of the alpine (downhill) ski resorts also have cross-country trails. Similarly, many of the dude ranches mentioned in this book become cross-country skiing havens in winter, with excellent, well-groomed trails. In many cases, you can begin skiing right from the lodge door.

Following is a small selection of cross-country touring centers which offer excellent facilities, in terms of rental equipment, lessons, and accommodations. This list is by no means complete, however; there are many more X-C facilities than can be described here. *Cross-Country Skier Magazine*, which is available monthly (from October to February), carries listings and advertisements for a wide variety of destinations. You might also want to pick up a copy of *Fodor's Skiing in North America* (Random House), available in bookstores and libraries. Although this is primarily a guide to downhill skiing, the information given for each major ski center indicates whether cross-country trails are available, too.

STEAMBOAT SPRINGS
Steamboat Springs, Colorado

There are a number of first-rate cross-country facilities in Steamboat Springs, among them *Vista Verde Guest Ranch*, which is described in detail on page 44. The Ranch has its own network of trails, 20 kilometers in all, winding through forests and meadows, across creeks and gentle slopes.

Also to be recommended in Steamboat Springs is the *Scandinavian Lodge*, with X-C trails beginning at the lodge door, and excellent Scandinavian food served at every meal. For instruction, the Ski Touring Center in Steamboat Springs is one of the best in the country. Many other accommodations are available in this quintessential western ski town, as well. For more information contact:

Chamber Resort Association, Box 774408, Steamboat Springs, Colo. 80477. Phone (303) 879-0740.

Vista Verde Guest Ranch, P.O. Box 465, Steamboat Springs, Colo. 80477. Phone (800) 526-7433.

Scandinavian Lodge, Box 5040, Steamboat Springs, Colo. 80487. Phone (303) 879-0517.

LONE MOUNTAIN RANCH
Big Sky, Montana

The United States National Biathlon team comes here every winter to train in cross-country skiing, and you can too. Forty-six miles of groomed trails and unlimited gorgeous scenery are all part of the winter package at this resort which doubles as a dude ranch in summer months (see page 46). Group lessons for beginners and private lessons for more advanced skiers are available at the ranch. Guided X-C ski tours to Yellowstone National Park are a highlight of each trip.

For more information contact: The Lone Mountain Ranch, P.O. Box 69, Big Sky, Montana 59716. Phone (406) 995-4644.

SADDLEBACK SKI AREA
Rangeley, Maine

If you want the geographical flavor of a western ski area in the East, try Saddleback. The mountains are higher than most other eastern peaks; consequently the Saddleback Ski Nordic Cross Country Center offers trials at higher elevations than most other New England sites. There are 50 kilometers of groomed trails. Families will be quite comfortable here, as the tempo is slow and the prices for meals and accommodations are reasonable.

For more information contact: The Saddleback/Rangeley Reservation Center, Box 317 K, Rangeley, Maine 04970. Phone (207) 864-5364.

TRAPP FAMILY LODGE
Stowe, Vermont

This is the home of the singing von Trapp family of "Sound of Music" fame. Unfortunately, the original lodge burned down a few years ago and has been replaced by an attractive glossier version. Nonetheless, an old world feeling persists. In the winter cross-country skiing is the focus, with first-rate instruction and well-groomed trails. Traditional Austrian fare is served in the dining room, and the views from the lodge are breathtaking! Rates include breakfast and dinner, and average $80 per night for adults, double occupancy. Rates are higher during the holiday season.

For more information contact: Trapp Family Lodge, Luce Hill Road, Stowe, Vt. 05672. Phone (802) 253-8511.

GARNET HILL LODGE
North River, New York

Great food, friendly people, and cross-country skiing from the door of the lodge are among the elements that make this authentic log house lodge well-known among X-C enthusiasts. You'll love the enormous garnet stone fireplace, and your children will enjoy the pool table and ping-pong table, which help to fill the nonskiing recreational hours. The Adirondack Mountain scenery isn't too bad, either.

Around the corner from the main lodge is a X-C ski shop where you can rent a complete set of skis, poles, and boots for $10 per day for adults and $7 for children. Group lessons cost $12 per hour; semiprivate are $15; and private are $19. A bonus is the hot chili that's always available in the ski shop for before or après-ski sustenance.

Room rates, including breakfast and dinner, range from $62-$87 per person, double occupancy, during the regular season. Rates are higher during the winter holidays.

For more information contact: Garnet Hill Lodge, Thirteenth Lake Road, North River, N.Y. Phone (518) 251-2821.

ON YOUR OWN

In New York City, every time a serious snowstorm strikes the area in the middle of the night, cross-country skiers are the first ones up and out in the morning. You'll see them with big smiles on their faces as they glide down the as-yet-unplowed avenues, heading toward Central Park. They know that the salt trucks aren't far behind, but for a few hours the wide, snow-laden streets belong to them. And when the streets are cleared, the parks are still a paradise. Cross-country skiing, in other words, is something you can do at the drop of a snowflake—anywhere.

If you live in or near a large metropolitan area in a northern state, you may be able to rent X-C equipment without going to a resort. Larger ski shops and sporting goods stores, especially those specializing in mountain sports, may rent you some skis, boots and bindings for the day. You can haul off to a park or, better yet, a golf course, where the snow is likely to be fairly undisturbed. Public golf courses are usually pretty tolerant of cross-country skiers; private clubs tend to be more territorial. Ask around to find out what the local customs are. Once you own your own skis, you'll be able to squeeze in a little X-C skiing whenever the snowfall is sufficient.

Once you've learned the basics and built up some stamina, you can head off to more remote and challenging locations, such as state parks, for an extended day's outing. Just remember that if you prefer groomed trails, you're better off at a ski touring center.

WATER SPORTS ADVENTURES

S afe, easy and wet—that's the nature of the water sports described in this chapter. You can take your pick from a variety of experiences—from canoeing, to whitewater rafting, to sailing and more. Each activity has its own charm and appeal, but they are all great for families who like to spend time on the water.

RIVER RAFTING: WHITEWATER AND OTHERWISE

There are two ways to enjoy the pleasures of traveling downriver on a raft with the majestic beauty of sheer rock cliffs and pine-laden forests towering overhead. One is to really "run the river" at high water—to confront the challenges of an almost out-of-control, human-against-nature situation, rushing through rapids so powerful that it might take a full-strength, six-person team to maneuver the raft safely.

A more enjoyable adventure for families, though, is the tamer alternative—a sometimes lazy, sometimes exhilarating float through the same spectacular scenery, with enough opportunity to get wet and cool off in the hot summer sun. Oh, you will still paddle furiously at times—to avoid a small but harmless boulder in the path. And you'll screech with mock fear at the amusement park-type thrills and chills of going through a tiny rapids or over a small falls. But the pace is much more comfortable, with those deliberately selected points of excitement punctuating an otherwise easy ride. At this pace, river rafting can be a fabulous family adventure.

Fortunately, most whitewater outfitters and raft trip organizers are not at all eager to take young children on the rough, tough trips. Minimum age policies and clearly stated warnings in outfitters' brochures make it fairly easy to tell which raft trips are right for your family and which ones are not. Nonetheless, it's a good idea to find out something about rafting before you select a trip, because you know your own children better than anyone else. Only you can really assess whether or not your 8-year-old is strong enough to hold onto the raft ropes during a rapids run, or whether your 12-year-old can swim well enough (with a life jacket on of course) to stay afloat until rescued if the raft turns over. This is a worst-case scenario, and on most family-oriented trips the raft is very unlikely to turn over. But the possibility exists, so you should remember that age guidelines are just that— guidelines. You've got to factor in what you know about your children to make an informed choice.

Here, then, are some tips to help you choose a river raft trip.

CHOOSING A RIVER

Part of the selection process includes choosing a rafting trip on the right kind of water. There are six classes of rivers from Class I, which has the easiest, calmest water, to Class VI, the wildest. Specifically, the classes are defined as follows:

Class I—Moving water, only a few small waves, and few or no obstacles.

Class II—Rapids of some difficulty in a wide, clear channel.

Class III—Numerous high, irregular waves; rocks and eddies; passages are clear, although narrow, and require skillful maneuvering.

Class IV—Long, difficult rapids, with powerful waves and turbulent water; dangerous rocks; precise maneuvering required; rescue can be difficult.

Class V—Extremely difficult, with long, very violent rapids; routes must be scouted from shore. Riverbed extremely obstructed; violent current, steep gradient. Very dangerous, with rescue almost impossible.

Class VI—Unrunable.

As you can see, Class I and Class II rivers are fairly tame, although you are likely to get wet going through Class II rapids. There are boulders which could become obstacles if no one in your raft had any sense of how to paddle or if you wandered far off course. Class III is challenging for beginners; you will *definitely* get wet in the course of running this river, and there is more risk than with Class I and II. However, Class III rivers are generally considered to be safe for adults, even for beginners. Whether an inexperienced family can handle a Class III river depends on the ages and general abilities of the family members. For anything beyond Class III, you should have some previous rafting experience. At certain times of year, notably spring when the water is at its highest, a Class III river will turn into a Class IV, and so on.

To choose a river for a family trip, you need to consider a lot about your children: their size and weight, their comfort in and around water, their stamina and endurance, their ability to cope in on-the-spot situations, and, of course, their ages.

RAFTING WITH CHILDREN: AT WHAT AGE?

In general, children from about the age of five and up can go rafting on a very calm river as long as you, the parents, are comfortable in the water. Unfortunately, few rafting outfitters offer trips of this nature, because rafting enthusiasts are usually looking for more excitement than that. If your children are primarily between the ages of five and eight, you may want to opt for a different kind of water sports adventure, such as canoeing. If you're determined to take young children rafting, there are a few outfitters listed later in this chapter which offer minifloat trips for children from age four or five and up; and there's one innovative outfitter who offers a daycamp program where younger children are tended to on shore while parents and older children hit the river.

For children 8 to 12 years old, there are perfect trips on Class I and II rivers, some of which have small areas of Class III rapids for a splashy ending.

From about the age of 12 on, most children can handle the same kind of mildly exciting whitewater adventure that first-time rafting parents can handle. In other words, they can handle the beginner trips where you're all in the same raft and are accompanied by an experienced guide. These are usually one-day trips, mostly Class II and Class III.

One final bit of advice for selecting a river or trip. Some of the *very* easiest trips which on the surface seem to be ideal for families and kids, are occasionally organized so that there's only one guide for every two or three rafts. This can be okay if the water is truly calm, but not so good in Class II waters or beyond because it means that *you* have to be responsible for too much at once: navigating your own boat, instructing your kids about paddling techniques and watching out for everyone's safety. So read the outfitters' literature carefully, choose a guided trip, ask a lot of questions and remember that you can always take another, more challenging trip if your first trip proves to be too easy.

ABOUT CHILDREN IN THE WATER

Rule number one: *Children must always wear life jackets.* In fact, everyone needs a life jacket on a raft trip. The rafting outfitter will most likely provide them, but if your child is very young, you should double-check ahead of time to be sure they'll have life jackets in his or her size.

Rule number two: *Never take your children river rafting in the spring or fall.* At those times of the year, even if the air is warm, the water is icy cold. And when you're whitewater rafting, you're bound to get wet. Young children are particularly susceptible to the effects of cold water, and they can start turning blue faster than you can say "I rafted on the Youghiogheny." So if your children are under 12 years old, plan all rafting trips, or any water adventures, for that matter, for the summer months of June, July or August. In the heat of a blistery August day, everyone in your raft, kids included, will be happily looking for ways to get thoroughly, totally drenched!

TYPICAL RAFT TRIPS

Most outfitters offer a range of trips from half-day and all-day guided trips to seven- or eight-day camping/rafting trips. You'll probably want to choose a one-day trip, unless your children are teenagers and you're looking for a full-scale wilderness experience.

In either case, you'll need to reserve your space on a rafting trip ahead of time. This isn't a spur-of-the-moment adventure, as most outfitters are booked up many weeks in advance. When making a reservation, you'll be asked to send a deposit which can only be refunded with sufficient advance notice. Be aware that rafting trips are rarely cancelled due to the weather. If it rains and you decide to stay home, don't expect to get your deposit back.

On the one-day trips, the group typically meets in the morning at the outfitter's base camp or a parking lot which may or may not be very near the "put-in" point. Often, the parking lot is near the "take-out" point, so that at the end of the trip, you can simply walk a few hundred feet to your car. If so, you will be shuttled by car, van or bus to the put-in. (With the other configuration, you park near the put-in, and then at the end of your rafting adventure, you're shuttled back to your car.)

On some trips, you may be required to help carry the raft to the water. Then, before getting into the raft, everyone in your group will be given some instructions by your guide. You'll learn the basics of paddling and the importance of following directions quickly when the guide gives a command. And then the fun begins!

Lunch is often provided by the outfitter on the more expensive trips, and sometimes the food is quite elegant. On cheaper trips, you bring your own. Either way, you'll have a picnic lunch at a scenic point along the river. Then it's usually back in the water to continue downriver until midafternoon.

At the take-out point, you'll sometimes find hot showers included in the package price, but check with the outfitters to be sure. There should also be a place to change into a set of dry clothes you've cleverly brought along and stowed in your car.

Some of the more sophisticated outfitters arrange dinner at this point as well, and often there will be photographs on display at dinner—pictures of YOU! Miracle of miracles, a photographer on shore has just happened to capture one of your most hilarious (or embarrassing, or triumphant) moments. Souvenir prints of these photos are available for an additional fee.

RATES: The average cost of a one-day guided rafting trip, with lunch or dinner, is about $75 per person for adults. Children usually receive a discount, and in some cases, children go free.

WHAT TO WEAR, WHAT TO BRING

In summer, which is the only time to be rafting with young children, you'll be most comfortable in a swimsuit or shorts, T-shirt, and a hat. You *must* wear shoes: Tennis shoes with laces are best, or you may be able to rent wetsuit booties from the outfitter. You need shoes to protect your feet from rocks if you fall overboard, and for those occasional times when it's necessary to stick out your foot and push off from the rocks. Thongs, boat shoes and flip-flops are *not* safe on a raft trip because they can come off too easily, go flying out of the boat. Then you're in trouble.

Don't forget sunscreen, a sun hat, a sport strap for eyeglasses, and towels and dry clothes to be kept in the car for use when the trip is over.

If the outfitter doesn't supply lunch, bring your own, packed in a plastic bag (to keep it dry). *Don't* bring any alcoholic beverages, glass or Styrofoam containers. *Do* bring a garbage bag for the trash.

In spring, fall, or anytime the weather is cool, you'll need warm, wool clothes and a two-piece foul weather suit or a wetsuit, which can be rented from the outfitter.

If it rains, the raft trip will probably not be cancelled. If you decide to go rafting in the rain, be sure to dress warmly, wearing wool clothing and a windbreaker or rain jacket on top. Or better yet, rent a wetsuit from the outfitter.

WHERE TO GO RAFTING

Following is a list of a wide variety of river rafting outfitters, with brief descriptions of their offerings. Some specialize in daredevil trips on Class V rivers, some feature once-in-a-lifetime trips down the Colorado River in the Grand Canyon, and some offer combination vacations: rafting/cycling, rafting/fishing, or rafting/horseback riding adventures. But all these outfitters also offer at least one simple rafting trip that's appropriate for parents with young children. If you're in an adventurous mood, send for *all* the brochures! You'll have a wild time just reading them.

IN THE EAST

UNICORN RAFTING EXPEDITIONS
Brunswick, Maine
Unicorn offers one-day rafting trips and overnight camping trips for families, on various rivers in Maine. There is a supervised day camp for children ages 3 to 11 at the Lake Parlin base camp. Minimum age for Kennebec River raft trip: 12 years old; for overnight riverside camping and rafting: 10 years old. For more information write Unicorn Rafting Expeditions, P.O. Box T, Brunswick, Maine 04011. Phone (207) 725-2255.

WHITEWATER CHALLENGERS INC.
White Haven, Pennsylvania
Summer rafting on the Lehigh River in northeastern Pennsylvania, two hours from New York City and Philadelphia, is the best bet for families. Brunch is included with their very reasonably priced one-day rafting trip. Minimum age for rafting: five years old. For more information write Whitewater Challenges Inc., P.O. Box 8, White Haven, Pa. 18661. Phone (717) 443-9532.

WHITEWATER ADVENTURES INC.
Ohiopyle, Pennsylvania
This is the home of two of the funniest names in whitewater rafting: Ohiopyle, Pennsylvania, and the Youghiogheny (pronounced Yock-i-gain-ee) River. But don't laugh: The Yough happens to have some of the best whitewater east of the Mississippi. Whitewater afficionados love the Class IV and V trips; your family will love the tamer stuff available on the Lower Yough. Minimum age for the Lower Yough is 12 years old. If your children are younger than that, you can rent a raft and paddle around on the Middle Yough, but don't expect flat water. The Middle Yough has enough whitewater to keep you busy. Minimum age for self-guided trips on the Middle Yough: four years old. I'd call this a PG situation, though: parental guidance suggested! Whitewater Adventures Inc. doesn't offer guided trips. For more information contact Whitewater Adventures Inc., P.O. Box 31, Ohiopyle, Pa. 15470. Phone (800) WWA-RAFT.

IN THE SOUTHEAST

WILDWATER EXPEDITIONS UNLIMITED, INC.
Thurmond, West Virginia

This is one of several outfitters offering guided raft trips on the New River in West Virginia. There are Class I and II beginner trips for families, and the package includes lunch, beverages, equipment and a guide. Minimum age: six years old. Also available are overnight camping trips, combination raft and horseback trips, guided bass fishing trips, coal mine tours and a fabulous (and expensive) one-of-a-kind chartered raft trip which includes transportation by helicopter to the river, gourmet dinner served riverside on fine china with selected wines, rafting, of course, and two nights of accommodations in a first-class resort. For more information write Wildwater Expeditions Unlimited, Inc., P.O. Box 55, Thurmond, W.Va. 25936. Phone (800) WVA-RAFT.

MOUNTAIN RIVER TOURS
Hico, West Virginia

Rafting on the New River in West Virginia, plus savings on motel accommodations, are two highlights of this outfitter's offerings. A variety of other deals, discounts and packages are available as well, including horseback riding and rafting combos. Children pay half price on Tuesdays all summer long. One call to the toll free number is all you need: They'll make all kinds of arrangements for you—even airline reservations. Minimum age for raft trips: 12 years old. For more information write Mountain River Tours, Box 88, Sunday Rd., Hico, W.Va. 25854. Phone (800) 822-1FUN.

SOUTHEASTERN EXPEDITIONS
Atlanta, Georgia

This outfitter offers rafting trips from two southeastern locations: the Chatooga River and the Ocoee River. The Chatooga River, which is two hours by car from Atlanta, is known as the filming location for the movie "Deliverance." Minitrips on a tame section of the Chatooga last 2½ hours each and are great for younger children. Minimum age: eight years old. The Ocoee River, with mostly Class III and IV rapids, offers a good deal more excitement in the same two-hour time frame. Trips on the Ocoee originate from the Ocoee Wildlife Management Area, about 30 miles from Chattanooga. Minimum age: 12 years old. Catered lunches and hot air balloon rides are also available. For more information contact Southeastern Expeditions, 2487 North Druid Hills Road, Atlanta, Ga. 30329. Phone (800) 868-7238.

NANTAHALA OUTDOOR CENTER
Bryson City, North Carolina

One of the most responsible, environmentally conscious and educationally-oriented outfitters in the country, Nantahala offers not only whitewater adventures but a whole range of outdoor sports activities. Their programs are top-notch and include such activities as rock climbing, canoeing, kayaking, river rescue, raft guide training, cycling tours and log cabin workshops. If you want to go rafting and kayaking in Nepal, this is the organization to contact. But you can also just stick to family rafting on the Nantahala River in the Great Smoky Mountains (minimum weight: 60 lbs) or on the French Broad River in North Carolina (minimum age: 10). For more information write Natahala Outdoor Center, U.S. 19W Box 41, Bryson City, N.C. 28713. Phone (704) 488-6900.

IN THE WEST

ACTION WHITEWATER ADVENTURES
Provo, Utah

In the West, things always seem to be on a much larger scale. The mountains are bigger, the rivers are wider, and sometimes the whitewater is wilder. Still, there are plenty of rafting opportunities for families.

Of this outfitter's offerings, the one- and two-day trips on the American River in California are well suited to families. Minimum age: none officially stated. Check with the outfitter for specific water levels during your intended vacation. For more information contact Action Whitewater Adventures, P.O. Box 1634, Provo, Utah 84603. Phone (800) 453-1482 or (801) 375-4111.

WHITEWATER VOYAGES
El Sobrante, California

Some of the most exciting rivers in Idaho, California, Oregon and Arizona are run by this outfitter. For families, the best trips are the South Fork of the American River and Cache Creek, both located in central California. The Cache Creek trip is the easier of the two, offering a "nice, easy, fun voyage through a canyon of absolute beauty." This trip is tame by most whitewater standards, but may be plenty challenging for one or two parents and a pack of small fry. The guided tour of Cache Creek rather than the paddle-your-own trip can make it even easier. Sumptuous meals are included as part of the package deal. Minimum age on a guided Cache Creek paddle boat trip: six years old. Minimum age on the South Fork of the American: seven years old. For more information write Whitewater Voyages, P.O. Box 906, El Sobrante, Calif. 94803. Phone (415) 222-5994.

KINGS RIVER EXPEDITIONS
Fresno, California

After mid-June, the water on the Kings River in central California warms up sufficiently and the water level drops, so this trip becomes ideal for families. Two meals are included in the package price of $86 per person on weekdays, $110 per person on weekends, with a small discount for children. Overnight camping trips are also available. Minimum age after mid-June: nine years old. For more information contact Kings River Expeditions, 211 N. Van Ness, Fresno, Calif. 93701. Phone (209) 233-4881.

DVORAK'S EXPEDITIONS
Nathrop, Colorado

Long known for its responsible approach to river running, Dvorak's is an excellent outfitter which provides rafting, canoeing, kayaking and fishing expeditions on 10 rivers, in 29 canyons and in 3 different countries. A solid and extensive track record of organizing trips for youth groups and special populations (handicapped and disabled, among others) has given Dvorak's Expeditions the edge in attracting families who are looking for week-long vacations. Two- and three-day trips are also available. Among the expeditions that are ideal for families are the Upper Colorado River and Lower Gore Canyon in Colorado; the Rio Chama Canyon in New Mexico; and the Hawaii trip. Younger kids go free on certain trips during specific dates.

Rates range from $55 per person for a one-day trip, to $558 per family for a three-day trip, to $995 per person for the one-week Hawaiian trip. There is no minimum age for children in an oar boat, which is a larger raft propelled by a guide using oars. Minimum age in the smaller paddle boats: 10 years old. For more information write Dvorak's Expeditions, 17921-B U.S. Highway 285, Nathrop, Colo. 81236. Phone (800) 824-3795 or (719) 539-6851.

SAILING

For people who like the water and love to feel the wind in their faces and smell the salty spray in the air, few adventures are as satisfying as a vacation spent on a sailing vessel. Sailing offers you the chance to look at the world from a different perspective and to escape from civilization without leaving all of the creature comforts behind. The scenery is usually magnificent and

the company onboard is almost always good because sailors are a special kind of people. They're gregarious yet private, fiercely individualistic yet very tolerant, strictly disciplined and at the same time relaxed. The sailors' attitude and the nature of the adventure create a wonderfully warm and welcoming atmosphere—one in which togetherness and teamwork are emphasized. There's no place for tension or competetiveness.

There are a variety of ways for you and your family to have a sailing adventure together, ranging from an intensive week at a sailing school off the coast of California, to an idyllic outing aboard a Maine windjammer, to a two-hour "environmental" sail aboard a Hudson River sloop in New York. Your choice will depend on your interest in learning how to sail, geographical preferences, budgetary considerations and the age of your children.

CHILDREN AND SAILING

Children tend to do well on sailboats when they are old enough to crew, or at least share some of the sailing responsibilities. At what age that happens depends a lot on the kids, and a little on the skipper's philosophy. Some boating people welcome children of any age; others really don't want to see your kids until they are teenagers. Keep in mind also that very young children tend to feel cooped up on a sailboat, where space is often quite limited. With children ages 8 to 16, it's a judgment call that will depend on your own kids' interests and temperaments.

A few words about clothing for sailboats: First of all, you need rubber-soled shoes to walk on the deck without damaging the boat or slipping on the potentially wet surface. If you don't have traditional waterproof boat shoes, rubber-soled tennis shoes will be fine. You should also remember that the air near the water is often much cooler than it is inland, so sweatshirts or sweaters are in order, even in summer. In the fall, plan to layer up, anticipating cold, chilly winds. And if there's the slightest possibility of rain, bring a hooded slicker or a raincoat and hat for each member of your family. Remember that once you're out on the water, there's no quick or easy way to take shelter from a storm.

Following are brief descriptions of the kinds of sailing adventures you might take, followed by specific outfitters or organizations offering the sails.

CHARTERED SAILBOATS AND SAILING SCHOOLS

An easy way to have a sailing adventure without overloading on the sport is to charter a sailboat for your family. Most marinas have skippered charter boats available, for trips of just a few hours or for a week or more. Sometimes you bring the supplies (food, bedding,and so forth), sometimes they are provided. If you charter a boat from an outfit that also offers sailing lessons, they'll often be willing to include some sail-training during your outing (see Sailing Schools, below). Or you can simply sit back and enjoy the ride.

If you're seriously interested in learning to sail, you might want to go one step further, and sign up the entire family for sailing lessons. Most sailing schools are located at a marina with a fleet of various-sized boats at their disposal. Typically, a beginner's course will consists of a total of about 15–18 hours of instruction, spread out over five or six days. Most of each lesson is spent on the water, but some concepts are easier to teach in a classroom with the aid of chalkboards and videotape equipment. This might not sound much like an adventure, but trust me: Spending three hours a day on a sailboat with an instructor who expects you to take charge of raising and lowering the sails, plotting the course, taking the rudder and more is *not* boring!

California Sailing Academy
Marina Del Rey, California

This organization, located on the California coast just south of Los Angeles, is equipped with a fine fleet of boats and many knowledgeable skippers/teachers who will happily tailor a sailing and teaching program to your level of interest. Given the academy's proximity to Disneyland and other Southern California attractions, you might arrange a combination vacation, with sailing as the main focus, but with time allotted for other activities as well. For instance, you could enroll in a week-long beginner's course, which costs $255 per person for a total of 16½ hours of training (about three hours each day), mostly on the water. Because the classes are always limited in size to about four people, a family of four would essentially be given private instruction. Another option is an intense onboard, week-long course—only appropriate for families with older kids and teens. You can also charter a skippered boat for a one-day sail at a cost between $150–$225 for a family of four. Flexibility is the password here. Whatever you want in the way of sailing experience, they'll make it happen. Minimum age: four.

For more information write California Sailing Academy, 14025 Panay Way, Marina del Rey, Calif. 90292. Phone (213) 821-3433.

SOUTHERN YACHT CHARTERS
Fairhope, Alabama

Despite the name, this group also emphasizes learning how to sail and will tailor a sailing vacation to your needs. You can charter a boat with a skipper for an evening, a day, three days, or more. On the longer trips you can live aboard ship, and take sailing lessons whenever the mood strikes you. Or you can let the skipper handle the boat while you fish, swim, and bask in the sun. These tours sail the waters from New Orleans to Panama City, Florida, passing and occasionally stopping at some of the whitest sand beaches you'll ever see in your life.

For more information write Southern Yacht Charters, P.O. Box 1492, Fairhope, Ala. 36533. Phone (800) 458-SAIL.

FORT MYERS YACHT CHARTERS
Fort Myers, Florida

This outfitter can arrange just about any kind of sailing adventure you want: lessons, day-sails with a captain, or longer voyages. And the climate in Florida being what it is, you can sail year-round, making this the perfect winter adventure for sun-starved Northerners.

For more information write Fort Myers Yacht Charters, 14341 Port Comfort Road, Ft. Myers, Fla. 33908. Phone (813) 466-1800.

MAINE WINDJAMMER CRUISES
Rockport, Maine

This is like nothing you've ever done before—unless, of course, you've done it before. Maine windjammers are very large sailing vessels of unparalleled beauty and majesty. Like the tall ships of old, they are crafted of exquisite woods and polished brasses, and capable of streaking through the waters of the Atlantic Ocean with amazing speed. As a guest onboard a windjammer, you'll eat bountiful meals, experience breathtaking sights, see more stars in the heavens than you can imagine, and enjoy great camaraderie with the other passengers and crew members. You may choose to help out with the sailing chores, or take a turn at the wheel. But you certainly aren't required to learn to sail or to pitch in on the sailing chores. It's up to you. Spend the whole time staring at the osprey circling overhead, or watching for whales to come gliding by if you prefer. You can also go ashore when your boat anchors at one or more of the many quaint seaside Maine towns or at a hidden island retreat.

Windjammer cruises are either a half week or a full week long, and leave from three ports: Camden, Rockport and Rockland. Although each of the ships is individually owned, the entire fleet is united through the Maine Windjammer Association, which is essentially a clearinghouse. Consequently, it takes just one phone call to bring a torrent of information to your mailbox.

Only a few of the ships welcome children on board: the schooner *Mercantile,* which accepts children from age 12, and the schooner *Nathaniel Bowditch,* which accepts children as young as 8. The minimum age on the rest of the fleet is 16. Rates vary with the season, but range from about $530 per person for a six-day cruise to about $325 per person for a three-day outing during the high season of July and August.

For more information contact the Maine Windjammer Association, P.O. Box 317P, Rockport, Maine 04856. Phone (800) 624-6380.

OUT O'MYSTIC SCHOONER CRUISES, INC.
Mystic, Connecticut

This outfit offers cruises much like the Maine Windjammer trips, but as the name says, they sail out of Mystic, Connecticut, instead of Maine. The town of Mystic is a tourist attraction in itself, with its authentic seaport village, shops and restaurants all picturesquely situated on Long Island Sound. A number of charter boats sail from these waters, including two schooners—the *Mystic Whaler* and the *Mystic Clipper.* Both are two-masted, gaff-rigged ships which sleep about 50 people in a variety of private cabins. (Unlike modern sailboats, gaff-rigged boats have four-sided sails typical of older sailing vessels.) One-day overnight "sneakaway" trips offer you an opportunity to sail the waters off southern Connecticut and the northern shore of Long Island. You can explore the ports of Sag Harbor, Greenport or Block Island, and eat two meals aboard ship before returning late the next afternoon. Three-day whale watches are also popular trips aboard these windjammers, and kids love the three-day "Pirate Sneakaway" to a secret island in search of buried treasure!

For adults, prices range from $89 per person for the one-day trips, to $599 per person for a five-day "sneakaway" cruise. Children ages 5–10 are welcome on one-day trips for half-fare. Children ages 10–16 accompanied by their parents can go on all trips, but they pay the full fare.

For more information contact Out O'Mystic Schooner Cruises, Inc. 7 Holmes Street, Mystic, Conn. 06355. Phone (203) 536-4218.

EDUCATIONAL SAILS

Over the past 10 years or so, as the environmental movement came of age, a number of individuals and groups saw an opportunity to combine their love of sailing with an educational message that might motivate others to support environmental causes. Following are descriptions of three such organizations that offer families the chance to do a little impromptu sailing aboard magnificent boats, learn about water environment issues, and perhaps contribute in some way to a worthwhile cause.

THE CLEARWATER
Poughkeepsie, New York

The *Clearwater* is a very special boat with an unusually dedicated crew. It offers a unique opportunity to sail the Hudson, a great and powerful river that flows 200 miles from the Adirondack Mountains in upstate New York to New York City. Sailing the *Clearwater* in the evening is an almost magical experience, with the Palisades rising majestically in the west and the sunset casting its golden glow.

Clearwater is the name of both a nonprofit environmental advocacy organization and its boat, a graceful 106-foot gaff-rigged sloop. Ever since the organization was founded in 1966, the focus of its activities has been to call attention to the environmental decay threatening the Hudson River. From April to November the boat takes school groups (during the day) and adults or families (at night) on three-hour educational sails. During the outing, you can help raise the one-and-a-half-ton mainsail, a job which requires the full effort of at least a dozen people. You'll also get to help with the trawl net, which brings aboard a sampling of river critters to be investigated with the boat's naturalists. You'll learn a little about water chemistry, check out the cabins and the galley below decks and take a turn at steering the boat. And you'll hear—and join in, if you like—some folk-singing and traditional music-making led by the *Clearwater* crew. The crew, by the way, is an exceptional group of committed, talented, open and affable, people who manage to make groups of strangers feel like family for the duration of the sail.

To participate in a sail on the *Clearwater,* you must be a member of the organization. Family membership is $35 per year, with much of the fee going to sustain various advocacy actions aimed at protecting the environment. Member sails are free and are scheduled mostly during the summer. Some sails originate from New York Harbor; others originate from other points north along the Hudson River. Sign up early, as the sails that originate in the New York City area are often in heavy demand. If you can't get on those sails, you might try signing up for a sail from a different location. In fact, it's a lot of fun—and more of an escape—to drive to someplace less familiar, like West Point for instance, and board the boat there. In any event, bring a picnic supper. And don't forget rain gear if there's any chance of rain—the *Clearwater* sails no matter what the weather.

Another adventure available to Clearwater members is the opportunity to join the crew and live aboard the ship for a week. This isn't something the whole family can do together, because Clearwater's policy is to gather a diverse group of people from different walks of life. But one parent and one child are often accepted together. And believe it or not, no sailing experience is required.

Volunteer crew members work hard on this outing, rising at seven a.m. or earlier to help prepare breakfast and do chores. The boat sails from about nine a.m. to noon, and the afternoon is spent doing everything from chopping firewood to cleaning the "head" (bathroom), and the work days are about 14 hours long. Children ages 10–15 are accepted with a parent; children ages 16 and older may volunteer alone. The cost of this adventure experience is phenomenally low: You are asked for a $25 donation to cover expenses for the week. Six volunteer crew members are selected each week by application.

For more information contact Hudson River Sloop Clearwater Inc., 112 Market Street, Poughkeepsie, N.Y. 12601. Phone (914) 454-7673.

FERRY SLOOPS
Hastings-on-Hudson, New York

This organization is a miniversion of the Clearwater example of building a sloop and using it to promote educational and environmental concerns about the Hudson River. Membership in Ferry Sloops brings with it a number of sailing opportunities, including specially scheduled member sails on the sloop *Sojourner Truth*. Members can also attend free sail-training classes, which are open to members in exchange for a few hours of work each week on the boat. Ferry Sloops' skippers and crew are the same sort of all-round wonderful people you'll find on the *Clearwater*, but since the organization is smaller, there's more opportunity here to develop long-term relationships. Annual membership for families is $20.

For more information contact Ferry Sloops, P.O. Box 534, Hastings-on-Hudson, N.Y. 10706. Phone (914) 478-1557.

Sound Experience
Poulsbo, Washington

It's not a coincidence that Sound Experience runs a program similar to the ones offered by Clearwater and Ferry Sloops. Morley Horder and Barbara Wyatt, founders of this fledgling environmental group, are former Clearwater people who decided to return to beautiful Puget Sound, taking their Hudson River experiences with them.

As of late 1990, the group offers its educational sails only in April and May, using a traditional sailing vessel owned and operated by another Puget Sound environmental group. Modeled on the Clearwater sails, these three-hour programs offer families and small groups a chance to experience the natural beauty of Puget Sound and to develop a sense of responsibility for it. Unlike Clearwater, however, this is not yet a membership organization; fees are charged for each trip. Adults pay $15 per person, children ages 9 to 13 are $10 each.

For more information, write to Sound Experience, P.O. Box 2098, Poulsbo, Wash. 98370. Phone (206) 697-6601.

CANOEING

Like rafting, the canoeing experience can range from the serenity of gliding on a shimmering lake or quiet river, surrounded by the never-ending reflections of trees and rocks and mountainsides, to the thrill-a-minute, spill-if-you-aren't-careful challenge of whitewater canoeing. Choosing the right river, then, is the key to having a great family canoeing adventure, just as in rafting. Bear in mind, though, that river rapids that are easy to run in a raft are much more difficult in a canoe, because you can't bash the canoe against the rocks without damaging it. In other words, pick a calmer river for canoeing than you would for rafting. (Read more about how rivers are classified on page 85 of the Whitewater Rafting section.)

Almost all of the canoe trips listed in this section are self-guided. That means that you won't have an expert along to help out if you get into trouble. It also means that you'll have to supply your own food and water for the trip. Be sure to take plenty of water since canoeing is strenuous exercise and you need to replace body fluids regularly.

Clothing requirements are fairly simple. Dress warmly if you're going in the spring and fall, and wear shorts or a bathing suit in midsummer. You and your children will need canvas shoes or boat shoes to protect your feet from rocks on the riverbed as you put in and take out the canoe. Hats, sunglasses, and sunscreen are also recommended for the summer months.

The minimum age for most canoeing, even the tame variety, is about 16 years old, since canoes tend to tip over easily if passengers fail to remain seated.

One last consideration for families who want to canoe together is the fact that most rental canoes seat two adults, with room for a child in the middle. So for a family of four or more, you'll need at least two canoes. If the children are young, the adults are likely to end up doing all the paddling. Still, canoeing is a wonderful activity, and a great way to introduce your children to such outdoors topics as tides, currents and respect for nature.

Following is a selection of canoe trip companies and some particulars on programs available for family canoe adventures. In general, most outfitters supply the canoes, paddles, life jackets, river maps, parking space and shuttles to or from the put-in location. Except where noted, you supply just about everything else.

NORTH STAR CANOE RENTALS
Cornish, New Hampshire

Great scenery, good fishing, historic covered bridges and picnicking on deserted river islands are all characteristic of canoe trips with this outfitter. Gliding down the pleasant Connecticut River, which marks the boundary between New Hampshire and Vermont for almost 250 miles, you'll see wildlife and waterfowl, and eventually pass beneath the longest covered bridge in America. Perch, bass and trout are abundant in these waters, so bring along a fishing license and gear. Trips of varying lengths are available, including half-day trips, full-day trips and overnight canoe/camping trips. Prices start at $10 per person for the half-day trip, and go up from there. Life vests, shuttles and all equipment provided. Also available is a combination canoe and bicycle package, with overnight accommodations at a Vermont inn.

For more information contact North Star Canoe Rentals, R.R. 2, Rt. 12A, Cornish, N.H. 03745. Phone (603) 542-5802.

POINT PLEASANT CANOE AND TUBE
Point Pleasant, Pennsylvania

Children are more than welcome at Point Pleasant Canoe and Tube, which offers several water sports activities on the Delaware River in Bucks County,

Pennsylvania. The Delaware has both flat water and areas of rapids, so you can take your choice. Canoe rentals are by the half-day, full-day or over-night, starting at $10 per person.

Another popular activity at Point Pleasant is "tubing" which involves float-ing lazily downstream on oversized inner tubes. The outfitter encourages children to try this sport, but parents should remember that small children get chilled very easily in cold water, even when the weather is hot. Small children can also slip out of the tubes or drift away from parents when the current is moving. If your children are younger than six or seven years old, you might consider putting them in a raft with an adult, while older children and other adults go tubing. Remember, too, that although the tubes them-selves are flotation devices, children (and nonswimmers) should wear life jackets, just in case they slip out of the tube.

A four-hour pedal and paddle combination package is available, in which you pedal to a given destination a few miles away and then paddle back. The bike trails are all off-road and run along the Delaware River and its canals. Pedal and Paddle packages cost $20 per person and are suitable for older children and teenagers.

For more information contact Point Pleasant Canoe and Tube, P.O. Box 6, Point Pleasant, Pa. 18950. Phone (215) 297-TUBE.

DOWNRIVER CANOE COMPANY
Bentonville, Virginia

This outfitter offers trips with a number of commendable features, including detailed maps of the Shenandoah River, the excellent fishing spots, and the sce-nic islands midriver which are great for picnicking. You have a choice of six dif-ferent trips from 3 to 19 miles in length, all of which can be completed in one day. The longest trips are for strong canoers in good physical condition, and are challenging even for them. The shorter trips are ideal for novices, and the water is mostly flat, with only a few Class I rapids. Rates range from $25 per canoe for the shortest trip, to $44 per canoe for the longest day trip. Overnight trips are also available. Rates include a shuttle to the put-in point, so that you finish your trip at the outfitter's base where your car is parked. It's nice not to have to wait for a shuttle at the end of a trip when you may be tired, cold and wet. Minimum age: six years old.

For more information contact Downriver Canoe Company, P.O. Box 10, Rt. 1, Box 256-A, Bentonville, Va. 22610. Phone (703) 635-5526.

REED'S CANOE TRIPS
Kankakee, Illinois

The Kankakee River, a clean, scenic Class I river with many small inlets and backwaters, is the setting for Reed's Canoe Trips. Birds, small animals and blooming wildflowers are in evidence throughout the summer, and the many islands make it possible to do some nature exploring en route. Fishing is said to be quite good in these waters, too, so if you want some catfish, crappies, bass, walleye or pike, bring along your fishing gear.

Reed's makes several trip itineraries possible, with put-in points determined by the length of the trip you want to take. Three of the most scenic outings pass by a riverside restaurant where you can stop for lunch. Overnight trips, with self-guided camping in Kankakee River State Park, are also available.

Rates for one-day trips range from $26 to $37 per canoe, with two people in the canoe. There is an extra charge of $2.50 for each additional child under 12. None of the trips begin or end at Reed's base camp, but shuttles to the put-ins and take-outs are included in the trip prices. Reed's also supplies a complimentary pamphlet about canoeing, with excellent illustrated instructions on paddling techniques and important tips on canoe safety.

For more information contact Reed's Canoe Trips, 907 N. Indiana, Rt. 50, Kankakee, Ill. 60901. Phone (815) WE CANOE.

BURKE'S CANOE TRIPS
Forestville, California

Located in the heart of Redwood country on the Russian River, Burke's is a small but well-organized business, offering canoe trips with wonderful scenery and the chance to just relax for a full day on the river. Wildlife is abundant, with osprey, blue heron, kingfishers, brown-horned owls, mud turtles and otter often seen. Courtesy buses stop by the take-out point every half hour to shuttle you back to your car. There's room in the canoe for an ice chest, so bring one along and plan to spend the day swimming, picnicking, sunbathing or just enjoying the unspoiled wilderness all around. The one-day canoe trip is $25 per canoe; each canoe will hold two adults and one or two small children. If your children are 10 or older, you'll probably need two canoes.

For more information contact Burke's Canoe Trips, Inc., 8600 River Rd., P.O. Box 602, Forestville, Calif. 95436. Phone (707) 887-1222.

CANOE USA

If you're looking for a week-long canoeing vacation in Vermont, Maine or Florida, look no more. Canoe USA has developed a variety of excellent tours in two basic configurations. You can canoe from inn to inn, spending each night in distinctive country inns or grand hotels and eating scrumptious gourmet food at every meal.

For another kind of outing, you can take a camping and canoeing trip where you supply your own sleeping bags and pads and Canoe USA brings everything else: food, camping equipment, elbow grease and know-how. This is a fail-safe way to learn camping—with a safety net of support from experienced group leaders, and the freedom to simply walk away and let someone else fix dinner if you're too tired to do it!

If you're seriously considering a canoe purchase in the near future, it's helpful to know that Canoe USA gives you the chance to try out different styles of canoes during every trip. In fact, they bring along more canoes than will be needed so that tour guests may try out various designs. And they are all Mad River Canoes, which are the top-quality canoes used by the most experienced athletes in this sport and that are of a much higher quality than the equipment usually provided by rental outfitters.

Minimum age for these trips is 12. Rates range from $249 per person for a three-day camping tour, to $859 per person for a five-day canoeing inn-to-inn vacation. There are no discounts for children.

For more information, contact Canoe USA, Box 610, Waitsfield, Vt. 05673. Phone (802) 496-2409.

FISHING

If you've ever stood on the end of a pier, dangled a line off the end of a bamboo pole in the water, and simply caught a fish, you'll probably disagree with my next statement: Fishing is a technical sport which requires a good bit of knowledge and even more enthusiasm to do well. The idea that an inexperienced family can slap together some fishing gear and head toward a river or lake for a day of spontaneous adventure is, honestly, a bit naive.

Still, it is possible for neophytes to have a family fishing adventure if they are determined to do so. There are a number of ways to go about this. You might investigate the fishing outings offered at some of the other vacation destinations listed in this book. Garnet Hill Lodge in North River, New York (see page 80), for example, features a series of ponds, rivers, and streams on a 50,000-acre wilderness area that will appeal to experienced fishermen and nature lovers alike. Lone Mountain Ranch (see page 79) has an excellent fishing program endorsed by Orvis, as do other dude ranches. Because many dude ranches are located in mountain areas, where the rivers run deep and the trout are frisky, they often promote fishing trips as a secondary attraction or even, in some cases, as an alternative to the usual horseback riding vacation package. And there are quality fishing trips on all the best-known rivers in the West offered by Dvorak's Expeditions, described in detail on page 93 as a first-class river rafting outfitter.

Most anglers who sign up for a full week of fishing at a resort like Lone Mountain Ranch are already accomplished at the sport. But you needn't be. The guides on these trips are experts who can teach you the basics. This is an expensive way for a family to learn fishing, however, and in all likelihood your children will lose interest before the week is up.

Another way to give fishing a try is to charter a boat for a fishing trip. Fishing charter operators supply bait and tackle, and some expertise about where to drop your lines. Some of the charter boats listed in the Sailing section on page 96 offer fishing outings. If you don't live near a lake or coastal area, boating and outdoors magazines are a good source for charters.

Many canoeing outfitters, including some listed in this book, are yet another source of helpful "where to" information about fishing. Although canoe outfitters don't usually rent or sell fishing gear, they often know enough about it to point you in the right direction.

And last, if you are the do-it-yourself type, you can check out a beginner's guide to fishing and simply plunge in. Your library will probably have a number of worthwhile books on the subject. But before you select one, you must first decide what kind of fishing you want to do. Are you interested in freshwater fish or saltwater fish? Pond and lake fishing, or stream fishing? Do you want to wade into the water in hip boots? Would you rather remain on a nice, dry pier? Or would you like to sit in a gently rocking boat?

To answer those questions, glance through a copy of *Fishing Basics*, by John Randolph (Prentice Hall). This is a simple overview of the various kinds of fishing: stream fishing, pond and lake fishing, inshore ocean fishing and offshore ocean fishing. Randolph explains (for the complete novice) the four kinds of fishing,and he also describes the techniques and equipment for each in a manner appropriate for the complete novice. Once you've mastered the terminology and sorted out the differences between saltwater fishing and freshwater fishing, you might read *A Basic Guide to Fishing for Freshwater Anglers of All Ages*, by David Lee (Prentice Hall). Lee's book is much more technically detailed and will give you an idea of just how much there is to learn about the sport.

One last book that is highly recommended: *Great Fishing and Hunting Lodges of North America* by A.J. McClane (Holt, Rinehart and Winston). This book provides a picturesque look at the kinds of fishing locations that true anglers dream about. It's a great resource for fishing vacation ideas.

Most important of all, you need to be aware of the fact that in all parts of the United States, fishing is regulated, which means you'll need to obtain a fishing license and a copy of the state's rules and regulations before you cast a line. Most states set strict limits on the size and number of fish you may keep, the seasons in which you may fish (especially for trout), and more. For information about fishing licenses and regulations in your area, contact your state's Fish and Game Department, or the U.S. Department of Natural Resources.

WILDERNESS ADVENTURES

In recent years, the wilderness, the earth and the environment have once again become topics of great concern for many Americans. The forest fires that ravaged Yellowstone National Park in the summer of 1988, the growing garbage problem and the arrival of parenthood for the '60s generation no doubt have contributed to a feeling among many people that they'd better take their children and themselves to see the wilderness while it still exists.

Fortunately, the wilderness hasn't vanished yet. It's out there, waiting to be explored by campers, hikers, backpackers and family adventurers. This chapter explores a number of ways to experience the great outdoors on your own or as part of a group; either as a traditional camper, or as a participant in family camps with environmentally oriented agendas and nature education adventures led by some of the oldest environmental organizations in this country.

NATURE VACATIONS, ENVIRONMENTAL ADVENTURES

A variety of wilderness experiences are available to families. Some of them emphasize educational programs, others concentrate on the physical challenges and still others focus on a sort of peaceful interaction with nature, with some sports activity included.

In addition to the trips described in this section, you may be interested in the environmental and educational organizations described in Chapter 6 under Sailing, namely Clearwater, Ferry Sloops and Sound Experience. Their efforts are primarily of an environmental nature, like the efforts of some of the following better-known activist groups.

One word of advice about selecting a nature trip for your family: Many of these trips are somewhat demanding, perhaps requiring participants to hike for several miles a day. They may not be appropriate for younger children. Carefully read the literature supplied by each organization, assess your own family's abilities and ask questions of the organizers if you are uncertain about the physical demands of a trip.

NATIONAL WILDLIFE FEDERATION: CONSERVATION SUMMITS

Each year the National Wildlife Federation offers four or five spectacular nature education programs called Conservation Summits. Held in a variety of locations such as Colorado's Rocky Mountains, the Pacific Northwest and Vermont's Green Mountains, these programs offer families a unique opportunity to learn about nature from professors and other experts, to explore the wilderness with a new perspective, to relax together and to develop a deeper appreciation of the outdoors.

As an adult participant in a Conservation Summit, you will design your own schedule, selecting courses in advance from a list of about twenty different subjects offered at each location. It's up to you to decide how much time you want for yourself and how much you want to spend in courses on such topics as orienteering, plant and wildlife ecology, outdoor photography, marine studies, birdwatching and geology. Children participate in high-quality comprehensive educational programs tailored to their age levels. Preschoolers, for instance, spend almost four hours each morning in a group that goes on minihikes and touch-and-feel expeditions, learns nature crafts and more. Children ages 5 to 12 join the Junior Naturalist program, which includes activities such as stream studies, bird walks, outdoor games, arts and crafts and folk tales. Teenagers are challenged by a ropes course, orienteering games and hiking.

In the afternoons and evenings, there are programs for the entire family—square dancing, sing-alongs and so forth. The summits are carefully designed with families in mind, so the mix of educational activities, group socializing and private time for family interaction is just right.

Each Conservation Summit lasts one week. Participants stay in dormitories or lodges, eating cafeteria-style meals with the group. Some summits have apartment-style accommodations available for larger families.

Rates are divided into two categories: the program fees, and meals and accommodations fees. The program fees are $200 per person for adults, $140 for children age 5 to 17 and $70 for preschoolers. The meals and accommodations fee varies depending on the location and style of rooms offered. On average, the cost is about $250–$300 per person for adults, $104–$159 per child. You must be a member of the National Wildlife Federation to participate in the Summits; annual membership is $15 per family.

If you're interested in a Conservation Summit, send for the NWF brochure and register as soon as possible. The size of each program is limited to about 550 total participants, and the programs fill up quickly. Each adult class is limited to about 40 people. Young children's classes are much smaller, with only 10–12 children assigned to a preschool group. For more information contact the National Wildlife Federation, 1400 Sixteenth Street N.W., Washington, D.C. 20036. Phone (703) 790-4363.

THE YELLOWSTONE INSTITUTE

Here's a chance to see Yellowstone National Park up close and through the eyes of an environmental specialist. The Yellowstone Institute, administered by a nonprofit organization called the Yellowstone Association for Natural Science, History, and Education, offers wonderful on-site courses taught to small groups who study and explore the park over a short period of time, usually three days. Of the nearly one hundred courses offered each summer, a handful are designed specifically for families to take together; half a dozen others are scheduled so that parents can enroll in adult courses given at the same time as their children's courses.

The courses have names like "Three Days at the Buffalo Ranch," "Geysers, Mudpots, and Hot Springs," and "Family Days: Exploring the Park with a Ranger Family," and have instant appeal for anyone who has dreamed of learning about Yellowstone's fascinating ecosystem.

Family course participants often choose to camp together in Yellowstone, although camping isn't required for enrollment in most programs. If you choose—and if you reserve early enough—you can stay at one of the well-known lodges or inns inside the park, or at a nearby motel. The Yellowstone Institute provides information about accommodations upon request.

Early registration for courses is advised, but even more important are lodging reservations, which are usually filled at least six months in advance. Course fees for a three-day family program are $80 for one parent and one child, plus $20 per additional family member.

For more information contact The Yellowstone Association, P.O. Box 117, Yellowstone National Park, Wyo. 82190. Phone (307) 344-7381.

WILDERNESS SOUTHEAST

How would you like to camp out under the stars on an island inhabited by wild ponies? Or creep along a pitch-black beach some warm night in July, waiting and watching for huge sea turtles to come ashore and lay their eggs? These are just two of the nature adventures possible along the coast of Georgia and South Carolina when you travel with Wilderness Southeast, a nonprofit educational corporation. The Sea Turtle Watch is a five-day affair during which you walk the beach for four hours each night as a volunteer researcher studying the sea turtle eggs, which are protected by the Endangered Species Act. After your nocturnal adventure, you sleep late in the morning in rustic, one-room dormitories on Fripp Island. To see wild ponies, you travel to Cumberland Island, off the Georgia coast, hike three to six miles each day and camp on the beach.

There are also canoe trips through the Everglades, or camping trips which include canoeing in rivers near Florida's Gulf Coast, and an Okefenokee swamp adventure which explores everything from the towering cypress forests to the sandy islands of the swamp. Each trip, which lasts one to seven days, offers a unique look at a natural wonder. The raw beauty of these places is heart-stopping.

Simple, nutritious and hearty meals are provided on all trips, and camping gear (sleeping bags, pads, daypacks, duffle bags) is available for rent if needed. Some trips are self-contained camping adventures, while other trips provide accommodations in cabins or aboard house boats.

Rates for a four-day trip through the Okefenokee Swamp, with all meals and cabin accommodations, are $345 per person for adults. The four-day Cumberland Island camping trips costs $250 per adult. On all trips, children receive a 15 percent discount when accompanied by one parent, 25 percent discount when accompanied by two.

The minimum age for some trips is 8, for others it is 12, 14, or 16. Be sure to check out the age requirements before you get your heart set on a certain adventure.

For more information contact Wilderness Southeast, 711 Sandtown Road, Savannah, Ga. 31410. Phone (912) 897-5108.

THE CHEWONKI FOUNDATION

Many organizations have a distinctive philosophy and a special way of looking at the world which permeates every venture undertaken. The Chewonki Foundation gives you a good idea of its philosophy in the brochure that describes its summer wilderness expeditions: "The expeditions are challenging—very little is worth doing unless it challenges—however they are not rigorous nor are they beyond anyone's reach."

Challenges and personal growth, along with outdoor skills and moral values that come from meeting challenges in the wilderness, are the essence of all the trips and workshops led by the Chewonki staff. The foundation, an outgrowth of the 70-year-old Camp Chewonki for boys in Wiscasset, Maine, offers wilderness trips, natural history workshops, coastal sailing trips on traditional sailboats, canoe trips and more. Flexibility is the key here. For example, you and your family might want to explore the arctic/alpine flora of Mt. Katahdin, a spectacular mountain in Maine's Baxter State Park. Or you might elect to attend a fly fishing workshop. Or join a canoe trip on the Allagash Wilderness Waterway. Chewonki encourages you to decide what you'd like to do and let them plan the program or trip in every detail.

Rates vary depending on the length of the trip and other logistical concerns. In general, however, trips costs average $60 per day, per person.

For more information contact The Chewonki Foundation, Wiscasset, Maine 04578. Phone (207) 882-7323.

SIERRA CLUB

Put away the pretty nature calendars and pack your bags. It's time to visit those gorgeously photographed wilderness locations you've been ogling all year, traveling in the company and capable hands of the Sierra Club, the people who brought you conservation issues long before they were fashionable.

Each year, the Sierra Club sponsors and organizes more than 400 trips, called Outings, in all parts of the United States and throughout the world. Guided by volunteer leaders—nearly 800 of them in all—Sierra Club members camp, canoe, hike, backpack and bicycle their way into the most remote regions, hoping to catch a glimpse of nature unawares. Instead of a glimpse, they usually get an eyeful: astonishingly beautiful vistas of sculpted mountain peaks, herds of caribou or waves of wildflowers blanketing a field. The range of opportunities is truly staggering. Only a handful of the Sierra Club trips are designed for families, but they even include programs that accommodate toddlers—hard to find among nature adventures.

The family outings vary from year to year, but in 1990 there were eight different trips, including two "Toddler Tromps" in Acadia Park, Maine, several hiking and camping trips in the Sierras, a Yosemite Park Toddler Adventure, and a Donner Pass Discovery near Lake Tahoe. The toddler trips even offer van transportation when needed during the trip, something that's virtually unheard of with other wilderness adventures.

Other family outings, however, are more strenuous. Nearly all trips require that members participate in meal preparation and other chores, reflecting the importance of cooperation in achieving group goals. Since many trips take place at high elevations, it's a good idea to acclimate for a day or so before the outing begins.

Rates for family outings range from $240 per adult for a week-long hiking trip among the redwoods of California, to $555 per adult for a week-long cabin stay at Stehekin Valley in Washington State. Children's rates for the same trips range from $160 to $370. All meals are included. You must be a member of the Sierra Club to participate in these programs. Be sure to inquire about age requirements for specific outings.

For more information contact Sierra Club Outing Department, 730 Polk Street, San Francisco, Calif. 94109. Phone (415) 776-2211.

CAMPING

Camping is a big subject. Entire books have been written on the how-tos and where-tos of camping. First-time campers would do well to purchase one of those and read it cover to cover. Strange as it may seem, camping is one of the most complicated activities described in this book. Certainly it requires more skills and knowledge than, say, horseback riding, lake canoeing, or bicycling.

One particularly good book on camping is *The Eddie Bauer Guide to Family Camping* by Archie Satterfield and Eddie Bauer (Addison-Wesley). It is out of print, but may be available at your local library. As you might expect, this book is particularly good for its exhaustive descriptions of equipment, although the book is nearly 10 years old and some extraordinary new materials have come along recently which aren't mentioned. Still, it's a fine guide and enjoyable reading. You'll especially enjoy the "Camper's Secrets" sprinkled throughout the book, which offer quick tips for camping success.

Another good book, also somewhat hard to find, is *Family Camping Made Simple* by Beverly Liston (Globe-Pequot Press). This is a book written by a woman who began camping when her children were very small, and has been camping ever since. Her insights about children and camping are excellent, and the book's appendix is a great resource. It contains 48 pages of campsite information, listing just about every state and federal agency you might want to contact about campgrounds.

More readily available is a good, solid guide called *The Complete*

Walker III by Colin Fletcher (Knopf). This is the hiker's bible, but campers can pick up plenty of detailed tips about camping gear and survival strategies.

Finally, you might want to send for one of the specialty catalogs from L.L. Bean. Because new materials are always being produced, and tents, sleeping bags and the like are always being updated, you'll find that many camping books are somewhat out-of-date soon after they're published. Catalogs, on the other hand, are filled with the latest gear. Just browsing through the pages of the L.L. Bean Spring Sporting Specialties catalog is a good way to construct a list of equipment you might need for a family camping adventure. To order a free catalog, phone (800) 221-4221.

CAMPING EQUIPMENT: WHAT YOU'LL NEED

Hold it right there.

If you're poised with your pencil and legal pad, ready to make a shopping list of camping gear based on the advice and information in this chapter, forget it.

What follows is an _overview_ of the kinds of stuff you're going to have to amass if you want to go camping—not a thorough checklist for you to follow. If you're crazy enough to set out on a camping adventure without reading a good book about the sport first, you can use this "think again" list as a reminder of some general categories of things you'd better be bringing along. But be sure to develop your own comprehensive list of camping equipment and supplies you'll need for your trip.

First of all, you'll need the traditional camping gear: tents, sleeping bags and pads, flashlights and/or lamps, cookstove with fuel, and cooking utensils including pots, potholders, bottle openers and tableware. You'll need enough food for the whole trip, plus drinking water or water purification tablets. You'll need a bunch of containers: coolers for the food, duffle bags for your clothing, garbage bags for the trash and a bucket or wash tub to wash dishes and clothing in. And that's just the beginning. (Do you need to buy a bigger car?)

Next you'll need to consider clothing. Clothing is an important item for campers, and with good reason. You need to plan for all kinds of weather—heat, rain and cold—which means you must take along a lot of things you might not use. A rain poncho should be on every camper's list, and most experts will tell you to take extra clothing, since you never know when you're going to get drenched. On the other hand, you should travel light, because everything has to be carried to the campsite. If you can somehow mesh those two pieces of advice, you will eventually become an expert camper yourself!

Don't forget survival equipment! This category includes knives, hatchets, fire-starters, maps, compass, a flashlight, whistles and a first-aid kit. In the "self preservation" category, you should pack sunscreen, insect repellent, hats, sunglasses and whatever you need for your sanity—chocolate bars or a guitar, for instance. Then there are the extras such as a camera, a reading book or two, field guides to birds and wildflowers and sports equipment (badminton set, frisbee or fishing tackle for example.)

Finally, be sure to pack that how-to book about camping—and double check your detailed "What to Take" list before you pull out of the driveway.

CAMPING WITH CHILDREN

If your children are all between the ages of 7 and 12, you probably don't have many concerns about taking them camping. This is the ideal age to enjoy the wilderness experience, and they're probably enthusiastic about the idea. But what about infants and toddlers? Can you really manage diapers in the wilderness? And how about teenagers? Will they complain about being away from their friends the whole time?

Most aspects of camping with a baby are quite manageable. In fact, infants and young toddlers are sometimes easier than older toddlers since you know how to cope with diapers. But children in the midst of, or just past, toilet training might have trouble coping with rustic "bathrooms," as they range from nonflushing outhouse-types to the somewhat grungy cement block bathrooms at many campgrounds. Of course, many other campgrounds maintain clean, tiled bathrooms and showers. If you use disposable diapers on your baby, all you need to bring along is extra garbage bags to store your refuse. Cloth diapers are a little more difficult, but can be washed out at the campsite and left to dry on a makeshift line if need be.

Some other issues of concern with babies and toddlers are:

▶ Insect bites: Be sure to protect your child with insect repellent on his/her arms and legs or clothing. Mosquito netting is also a good idea in the wilderness. It can be used to cover your baby in the stroller or car seat, which you'll probably want to bring to your campsite. Also, bring along a topical ointment to relieve the itch if someone gets bitten.

▶ Sleeping arrangements: Bring waterproof pads to protect the sleeping bags. Consider borrowing or buying a portable crib for your

infant as it can double as a playpen in the daytime. Toddlers will probably go to sleep easily at night on a camping trip, since everyone usually sleeps together in one tent.

▶ Safety: Everything is unavoidably on the ground, within easy reach when you're camping. Unfortunately that means that campfires, knives, hatchets, and propane canisters for the campstove are all hazards for little ones. You'll have to be especially attentive if you camp with children between the ages of nine months to three years. You might want to bring along an extra cooler with a lock, to use as a storage compartment for dangerous items.

▶ Naps: Most babies will sleep anywhere. But it's hard to get toddlers to sleep in the middle of a hot afternoon, especially when the camping experience is so stimulating. For this reason, you might want to bring along a small cassette recorder and tapes of your toddler's favorite bedtime songs or stories. Sometimes something familiar that reminds your child of home may be calming enough to trigger the napping mechanism. At least, you can always hope so!

Teenagers are another story entirely. They usually fall into one of two categories: those who *really* don't want to go camping, and those who are totally gung ho about the idea. The trick is to turn the former group into the latter, through careful presentation of the camping concept. With teenagers, you can often enlist their enthusiasm if you let them be part of the decision-making process. Rather than announcing at dinner one night, "Guess what? We're going camping!" you might show your teenagers some campsite literature or brochures, ask them how they feel about camping and involve them in the process of choosing a camping destination. Let them select an activity, such as boating or canoeing, to be included on the agenda. Teenagers are also usually much happier if they have their own tent. And you might want to let each teenager bring a friend.

CABIN CAMPING: AN EASY ALTERNATIVE

If you're not quite sure whether your family is tough enough to rough it, you might want to try an alternative, one that lets you gradually explore the camping concept. That is, you might want to take a family trip to a state or national park and stay in one of the cabins that are available. Cabin camping is ideal for families who want a wilderness experience, who want to live more simply then they do at home, but aren't ready to plunge into a full-fledged tent camping experience the first time out. Many hard-core campers would not call this form of vacation "camping" at all, but it makes sense for the novice.

Here's how it works. First, you contact a state or national park and ask for information about renting cabins. Many parks have a range of cabins available—everything from cottages that have fully equipped kitchens, full baths, and linens provided, to "tent cabins" which provide only a roof, a light-bulb, and some cots or bunks on which to put your sleeping bags.

Whether you choose the more rustic accommodations or not, you can acquaint yourselves with the wilderness and try out some of the camping skills you would need if you were *really* on your own. For instance, you can take a campstove with you and try cooking a full day's meals outdoors, rain or shine. If your cabin has a fully-equipped kitchen, you won't have to pack your own pots and pans from home, but you should keep a list of what you use on the campstove cookout so you know what to bring if you decide to try tent camping later. Or you might decide to build a campfire, not to cook on but simply to practice fire-building skills. Or wash your dinner dishes in a bucket outside with water you've carried from the lake. You'll also learn a lot about what clothing to bring on a camping trip.

Check out the tent campsites while you're in the park. Look at the bath-room facilities, observe the physical layout, and try to imagine spending a night there. It will give you a much better picture of camping than you'll ever get from this or any other book.

The fees for cabins owned and operated by state parks are usually quite reasonable. Fully-equipped cabins can be rented for as little as $28 per night. Bare cabins and "tent cabins" are less common, but cost as little as $18 per night for two people. Sometimes there is an additional charge for extra people. For information about cabins in state parks, contact the appropriate state Department of Parks and Recreation. For information about cabins in national parks, contact the National Park Service in Washington, D.C. Addresses are listed in the Appendix of this book.

Another option to consider, available from Kampgrounds of America (KOA), the national chain of private campground facilities, is the "Kamper Kabin." These are bare cabins, usually bunkbeds and electric-ity, so you must bring your own linens, sleeping bags, cooking gear— the works. Rates vary, but Kamper Kabins average $25 per night for two people, $2.50 for each additional person. The price is steep considering that you can get a completely furnished and equipped cabin in some state parks for the same money. The nicer KOA campsites often offer additional recreational activities, such as paddle boats, miniature golf, swimming, boating and so forth, for an added fee. The Yellowstone KOA, for example, located only six miles from the national park, has a game-room, provisions store, playground and miniature golf course on its grounds, with trout fishing, hiking and horseback riding nearby.

You may also want to try recreational vehicle (RV) camping, which shares many elements with cabin camping. In an RV, you pretty much carry all the comforts of home with you into a national park or commercial campground. Living and traveling in an RV isn't really camping, but many people enjoy it as an economical way to see the country and spend time *near* the wilderness, if not actually *in* it. Various sizes and shapes of RVs are available for rent, with advantages and disadvantages to each. Pop-up trailers that can be towed behind ordinary cars offer the most tent-like environment because, once set up, their soft, canvas sides can be unzipped to reveal many windows and screens. The pop-ups are a bit cumbersome and time-consuming to set up, and they have limited space; you must carry most of your gear in the car. Hard-sided trailers, by contrast, are easier to use, but the trade-off is that you don't get nearly as much fresh air circulation.

For more information about renting an RV or trailer, contact your local recreational vehicle dealer.

WHERE TO CAMP

There are thousands of campgrounds in the United States, many privately owned and many developed by state or federal agencies. Some are very primitive, with nothing more than a clearing and perhaps a firepit. At the other end of the spectrum are the very modern campgrounds which are geared toward people in RVs, and have water and electrical hook-ups, showers, laundry facilities, flush toilets and recreational facilities. At public campgrounds, tent campsites are often side by side with the RV campsites, which means that tent campers must endure whatever reminders of civilization their neighbors have chosen to bring along. Bright lights, radios, the hum of RV generators and even the chatter of television are never far away at campgrounds which cater to RVs.

Rates for campsites very enormously. Those owned by the government are less expensive or even free; privately owned campsites can cost as little as $4 per night or as much as $20. In many cases, particularly in the national parks, you'll need to make reservations well in advance.

In general, if you're looking for a wilderness experience, you'll probably be happier at a campsite developed by a state park, national park, the Forest Service or the U.S. Corps of Engineers. Those campsites are more remote, and consequently tend to be frequented by people who have come in search of peace and quiet, rather than those who are merely looking for a convenient place to park their vehicle not too far from the highway. Remember, however, that the farther you are from civilization, the longer the ride to a carryout store for more hot dog buns or a gallon of milk. It's also farther to the nearest hospital, in case of emergencies.

If you're willing to tolerate the company of other campers, who, after all, can be fairly decent folk, then a privately owned campground might be a good choice. It will offer convenience, recreational opportunities and a safety-net—if you find that you forgot to pack the matches, for instance.

The two best resource guides for information about campgrounds are the _Campground and Trailer Park Guides_ published by Rand McNally and revised yearly and the state-by-state campbooks available free to members of the American Automobile Association (AAA).

A wealth of information is available from the government agencies that administer the various national parks and wilderness areas across the country. Be sure to contact the National Park Service, the U.S. Army Corps of Engineers, the U.S. Forest Service, and Kampgrounds of America (KOA); their addresses can be found in the Appendix on page 133. The various state Departments of Parks and Recreation, and state Departments of Tourism are also helpful. When you write, be sure to indicate that you are interested in receiving maps, brochures and literature about camping.

S ome experiences are so special they belong in a category all their own. If you're looking for an unforgettable, one-of-a-kind adventure, look no further. Here are three unique opportunities that your children—and you—will remember the rest of your lives.

VIKING AFLOAT: CANAL BOAT TOURS

Unlike most of the water sports adventures available in the United States—thrilling whitewater trips on the Colorado River, or windjammer cruises off the rocky, romantic coast of Maine—the most popular water adventure in Great Britain is a bit tame by comparison. No daredevil skills are required; no risk to life or limb is involved. But it's a unique adventure, ideally suited to families of any size and children of any age.

What is it? It's a canal boat cruise or, as the English would say, "narrowboat holiday" through the canals that permeate the English countryside. Yes, there are canals in England, and there are special boats built which navigate them. The canals were dug in the late 1700s to facilitate commerce between English cities. At the time, no one suspected that the railroad would soon come along to spoil all the fun, so an extensive network of canals was built linking virtually every small town in the country with the larger postindustrialized cities. The canals thrived for about 75 years, until competition from the railway companies eliminated the demand for canal boat transportation. From the 1860s until just after World War II, the canals were defunct.

After the war, someone hit on the idea that since the canals were no longer used for commerce, they might be very pleasant to float upon to meander through the English countryside. The canals were nationalized, narrowboats for pleasure were built, and a whole new kind of adventure vacation was born.

Today, a trip on an English canal boat is both restful and involving. The boats themselves look something like long, narrow houseboats, with cabins which aren't exactly "below deck" so much as they are enclosed living spaces. You live aboard ship and captain your own boat, not a particularly difficult task as the boats are generally confined to narrow canals, so you can't wander off course or get lost and go no faster than four miles per hour! The unique challenge in piloting a canal boat is the fact that you must open and close a number of locks, or underwater "gates," as your journey progresses, in order to move from high water to lower water or vice versa. Some stretches of the route may have only one lock every mile or so, but other sections may have five or more locks in one mile.

At each lock, an adult must hop off the boat and work the apparatus which opens the gate, allowing the boat to enter the confined lock area. Then a sequence of steps must be followed to either fill the lock or empty it, thereby bringing the water level up or down to match the section of canal you are headed towards. Working the locks is the primary activity on a canal trip, and most people begin to look forward to each lock as they approach it. This isn't an adventure for lazybones, as some of the locks require a bit of muscle power and the job can become repetitious. But the kids can help, especially if they are, say, 12 years old and up.

When you tire of working locks and floating along so lazily, you simply moor the boat at the side of the canal and set off to explore one of the charming English towns nearby. In most cases the towns are right there, beside the canals, with shops, pubs, restaurants and general stores ready to feed your hungry and curious passengers. You can buy provisions, visit a local cathedral, and talk with friendly residents or get a look at their flower-filled English gardens before returning to the boat and heading on your way. The route is up to you and the pace is your own. The only requirement is that you reach your final destination, at the tour operator's headquarters, by the end of the week.

Since the boat is traveling very slowly, it's easy to walk along beside it on the canal bank, and people often do. Towpaths or footpaths parallel the canals for much of the way, allowing children to play in the grass or ramble along beside the boat as it progresses. Everyone must be onboard when you go through a tunnel, however, which is another exciting part of the trip, as most of the tunnels are quite low and spooky.

Small children, even toddlers, are fine on canal boats in part because so much of the boat area is enclosed, although a rambunctious toddler might fall overboard, or might run over the riverbank edge and leap into the canal from the towpath. As a precaution, you can tether your very small children with harness and long cord. Of course, all children should wear life jackets, which are provided by the boat company.

Boats vary in size and in the number of people they will accommodate, but all have essentially the same equipment and amenities: one or more sleeping berths, a galley with stove, refrigerator and dining table, closets, showers, flushing toilets and a small uncovered deck space with seats. Each boat is also equipped with hot and cold running water, central heating, lighting, radio, and electrical outlets for other appliances. It's a self-contained environment, in other words—something like a small floating condominium, although not quite so luxurious. The smaller boats sleep two people, and are about 35 feet long by 6 feet wide. Larger boats sleep six or more people, and are 60 or 70 feet long by 6 feet wide.

When you arrive for your vacation, the boat will be ready, even stocked with an initial supply of groceries if you desire, for which you will pay extra. The tour operator will teach you how to handle the boat and work the locks. He will also sell you excellent tour books with maps of the canals, lock locations, and detailed information about each town on the route. It's a good idea to order these books in advance, so that you can plan your route (and day-dream about your trip) before you arrive in England.

RATES: A week-long canal boat cruise for a family of four will cost between $375 and $600 depending on the size of the boat and time of year, with summer months being the high season. All fuel costs are included in the package rate. Air and ground travel to the two cruise locations, Worcester and Whitchurch, is not.

FOR MORE INFORMATION: Contact Viking Afloat Limited, Lowesmoor Wharf, Worcester WR1 2RX, England. Or telephone 011-44 (0905) 28667/8. Your best bet is to contact a travel agent who can help you make arrangements for everything: the canal boat tour, air transportation from London to either Worcester or Whitchurch.

HOT AIR BALLOONS

For sheer romance and glamour, few experiences can match a flight in a hot air balloon. Gently rising above the treetops and floating over the countryside with no particular destination in mind—in fact, no control over destination—your balloon will take you wherever the winds want you to go. You'll watch the sun rise or set, gaze down at rolling green fields or golden pastures, and experience the exhilarating sensation of silent motion high above the earth. If you've brought a camera, you can take photographs that will astound your friends. And if your pilot is skillful, he can lower to a cruising distance just above the treetops, the lowest point at which balloons can fly and the height of adventure in hot air ballooning.

Hot air balloon rides are always scheduled for sunrise or sunset, not for aesthetic reasons but because that's the only time of day when it's safe to fly. The balloon is at the mercy of air currents which accelerate and become more turbulent as the sun warms the air. At midday, the air currents are strong and unpredictable. By contrast, in the early morning and late evening, the air is usually calm.

If you're particularly concerned about safety, you'll probably want to schedule your family's balloon adventure for sunrise, the earlier the better. Morning flights tend to be slightly less turbulent, although the wind does pick up as the sun rises and the flight progresses. Sunset rides are just the opposite: you may take off during a slightly windy period, but as the sun goes down, the wind will calm down, too, and your landing will be an easy one.

A typical "champagne balloon ride" begins in an open field, a parking lot, or a park when you climb into the wicker basket—and yes, the baskets are still made of wicker, because it absorbs the shock on landing better than other materials do. On average, the ride will last about an hour, but *where* it ends is anyone's guess. The pilot can control the altitude of the balloon, but not the direction. When it's time to land, the pilot looks for an open spot and begins to descend, either by simply letting the balloon cool or by actually releasing some of the hot air through a vent. Ideally, you should come down slowly in an open field with no nearby electrical wires, trees, buildings or other obstructions. On landing, you will enjoy the traditional champagne toast, a custom which began years ago as a way of thanking the farmer or landowner on whose property the balloonist had descended.

Hot air ballooning is a thrill for adventurous-minded adults and older children, but it is not for everyone. Small children are almost always frightened by the noisy blast of the propane burners, which must be fired for 10 seconds every minute or so. Safety is also a consideration, as you've got to be able to follow instructions from the pilot in order to prevent injury on landing, and small children just aren't old enough for this responsibility. In most cases, the instructions are simply a matter of holding on tight and bending your knees, or supporting yourself on impact. From the age of about seven or eight, most children can manage the landing, but younger children can't.

Like many sports adventures, ballooning does involve some risks, among them is the possibility that the propane burner will fail during a trip, requiring a crash landing. But this kind of emergency is extremely rare. The greatest danger is choosing an inexperienced or irresponsible pilot, or one with bad judgment. All balloonists must be licensed by the F.A.A., but that may not be enough. You should look for a pilot who is cautious enough to cancel a flight if the weather conditions are not optimal, and who has flown enough to be able to accurately assess the speed of the balloon when underway.

So how do you select this balloonist? Ask a lot of questions when you contact a hot air balloon company. Ask how long the pilot has been flying, how much insurance the company carries and how long the company has been in business. Ask about age limitations for children, and use this as an indication of the balloonist's attitude toward safety. It's not that four-year-olds can't safely ride in balloons, but a company that refuses to allow very young children to fly is demonstrating greater concern about passenger safety. Ask about the possibility that your flight may be cancelled due to weather conditions—and be reassured to hear that it might be. And if you're super-conservative, you might even want to check with the nearest Flight Service Station to get your own official reading on the weather conditions for balloon flight on the morning or evening of your trip.

RATES: The cost of a hot air balloon flight averages about $125 per person, with some discounts available if your children don't weigh much. Weight is an issue with children because the pilot needs less propane to lift the basket. Some balloonists fly four-passenger balloons. Others fly only the smaller balloons which accommodate a pilot and two passengers. In that case, a family of four might want to try a "Hop and Pop" trip—a trip in which two family members go up, while the other two join the chase team on the ground, which follows the balloon's flight. After about half an hour, the balloonist descends and the family members switch places with the original chase team taking a 30-minute balloon ride while the first two join the chase.

FOR MORE INFORMATION: Information about commercial hot air ballooning can be found in the yellow pages under "Balloons, Hot Air." Or contact the Balloon Federation of America, Suite 430, 821 15th Street N.W., Washington, D.C. 20005.

BATS AND CAVES

For the past 14 years, Alan Cressler has been sneaking around in something like 8,000 different caves studying bats. Want to join him? It's cheap and easy, and obviously the kind of unusual opportunity that most people take advantage of only once in a lifetime. Through the auspices of High Country

Outfitters, an outdoor sports equipment retailer based in the Southeast, Cressler offers two-day trips to various caves in Georgia, Alabama and Tennessee. Cressler is a member of the National Speological Society, founded for the study of the underground, and his slant is decidedly that of the conservationist. "People think that just because caves are below ground, it doesn't matter what you do to them," Cressler says. "But that's not so." He believes that, like wilderness areas, caves are an endangered environment that should be protected and preserved.

Once a group has signed up for a caving expedition, Cressler likes to meet with the participants, to evaluate their experience. If you and your family are avid, able rock climbers, he might choose to take you into a cave that requires some vertical climbing. On the other hand, if you are complete novices in all such matters, Cressler knows a great many caves that he calls "tourist caves," which are perfectly safe for inexperienced adventurers.

What will you see in the caves? Bats, of course, and possibly crayfish or salamanders. You might also see rock formations, and there's definitely a lot of darkness. Many caves have "rooms" that are 100 feet high and wide. Others have long passageways, perhaps two miles long. Cressler will prepare you for the experience in the precaving orientation meeting by showing slides and talking about the world of the underground. He'll also address the issue of safety. "Many people, when they think about caves, think about things falling on them," Cressler says. "But that just doesn't happen." The only significant danger is the possibility of slipping and falling on the wet, slick surfaces. For that reason, Cressler requires that you wear hiking boots or some other kind of shoe with a ridged sole that will grip rock surfaces. If you don't have the right shoes, he'll take you to the "super-tourist" caves, where the chances of slipping are minimal.

Cressler also supplies helmets with lights attached, while you bring additional light sources, such as flashlights. He suggests that you wear some kind of gloves to protect your hands. You must provide your own camping equipment, food and transportation; Alan seeks out bat-filled underworlds and provides the expertise to penetrate their murky depths. Because the trips are tailored to individual participants, each trip is different, but all involve camping on Saturday night and traveling by van to a variety of cave locations in the Southeast.

RATES: The two-day trip costs $75 per person. You can also rent camping gear from High Country Outfitters for an additional charge.

MINIMUM AGE: High Country recommends that children be at least 12 years old, but younger children with hiking experience may participate with permission of the trip leader.

FOR MORE INFORMATION: High Country Outfitters, 595 Piedmont Avenue, Suite D203-1, Atlanta, Ga. 30308. Phone (404) 892-0828.

APPENDIX

NATIONAL FOOTBALL LEAGUE

American Football Conference

Buffalo Bills
One Bills Drive
Orchard Park, NY 14127
(716) 648-1800

Cincinnati Bengals
200 Riverfront Stadium
Cincinnati, OH 45202
(513) 621-3550

Cleveland Browns
Tower B, Cleveland Stadium
Cleveland, OH 44114
(216) 696-5555

Denver Broncos
13655 E. Dove Valley Parkway
Englewood, CO 80112
(303) 649-9000

Houston Oilers
6910 Fannin Street
Houston, TX 77030
(713) 797-9111

Indianapolis Colts
P.O. Box 24100
Indianapolis, IN 46253
(317) 297-2658

Kansas City Chiefs
One Arrowhead Drive
Kansas City, MO 64129
(816) 924-9300

Los Angeles Raiders
332 Center Street
El Segundo, CA 90245
(213) 322-3451

Miami Dolphins
Joe Robbie Stadium
2269 NW 199th Street
Miami, FL 33056
(305) 620-5000

New England Patriots
Sullivan Stadium
Route 1
Foxboro, MA 02035
(617) 543-7911

New York Jets
598 Madison Avenue
New York, NY 10022
(212) 421-6600

Pittsburgh Steelers
Three Rivers Stadium
300 Stadium Circle
Pittsburgh, PA 15212
(412) 323-1200

San Diego Chargers
San Diego-Jack Murphy Stadium
P.O. Box 20666
San Diego, CA 92120
(619) 280-2111

Seattle Seahawks
11220 N.E. 53rd Street
Kirkland, WA 98033
(206) 827-9777

National Football Conference

Atlanta Falcons
Suwanee Road at I-85
Suwanee, GA 30174
(404) 945-1111

Chicago Bears
Halas Hall
250 North Washington
Lake Forest, IL 60045
(312) 295-6600

Dallas Cowboys
Cowboys Center, 1 Cowboys Parkway
Irving, TX 75063
(214) 556-9900

Detroit Lions
Pontiac Silverdome
1200 Featherstone Road, Box 4200
Pontiac, MI 48057
(313) 335-4131

Green Bay Packers
1265 Lombardi Avenue
Green Bay, WI 54303
(414) 494-2351

Los Angeles Rams
2327 West Lincoln Avenue
Anaheim, CA 92801
(714) 535-7267

Minnesota Vikings
9520 Viking Drive
Eden Prairie, MN 55344
(612) 828-6500

New Orleans Saints
6928 Saints Avenue
Metairie, LA 70003
(504) 522-1500

New York Giants
Giants Stadium
East Rutherford, NJ 07073
(201) 935-8111

Philadelphia Eagles
Philadelphia Veterans Stadium
Broad Street and Pattison Avenue
Philadelphia, PA 19148
(215) 463-2500

Phoenix Cardinals
P.O. Box 888
Phoenix, AZ 85001
(602) 967-1010

San Francisco 49ers
4949 Centennial Blvd.
Santa Clara, CA 95054
(408) 562-4949

Tampa Bay Buccaneers
One Buccaneer Place
Tampa, FL 33607
(813) 870-2700

Washington Redskins
P.O. Box 17247, Dulles Airport
Washington, D.C. 20041
(703) 471-9100

MAJOR LEAGUE BASEBALL

AMERICAN LEAGUE

Baltimore Orioles
Memorial Stadium
Baltimore, MD 21218
(301) 243-9800

Boston Red Sox
Fenway Park
4 Yawkey Way
Boston, MA 02215
(617) 267-9440

California Angels
Anaheim Stadium
2000 State College Blvd.
Anaheim, CA 92806
(714) 937-6700

Chicago White Sox
Comiskey Park
324 West 35th Street
Chicago, IL 60616
(312) 924-1000

Cleveland Indians
Cleveland Stadium
Boudreau Blvd.
Cleveland, OH 44114
(216) 861-1200

Detroit Tigers
Tiger Stadium
Detroit, MI 48216
(313) 962-4000

Kansas City Royals
1 Royal Way
Kansas City, MO 64129
(816) 921-2200

Milwaukee Brewers
County Stadium
Milwaukee, WI 53214
(414) 933-4114

Minnesota Twins
501 Chicago Avenue S.
Minneapolis, MN 55415
(612) 375-1366

New York Yankees
Yankee Stadium
Bronx, NY 10451
(212) 293-4300

Oakland A's
Oakland Coliseum
Oakland, CA 94621
(415) 638-4900

Seattle Mariners
411 1st Avenue S.
Suite 480
Seattle, WA 98104

Texas Rangers
Arlington Stadium
1200 Copeland
Arlington, TX 76010
(817) 273-5222

Toronto Blue Jays
The Skydome
300 Esplanade West
Suite 3200
Toronto, Ontario M5V 3B3
(416) 341-1000

NATIONAL LEAGUE

Atlanta Braves
Atlanta Stadium
521 Capitol Avenue
Atlanta, GA 30312
(404) 522-7630

Chicago Cubs
Clark & Addison
Chicago, IL 60613
(312) 404-2827

Cincinnati Reds
100 Riverfront Stadium
Cincinnati, OH 45202
(513) 421-4510

Houston Astros
The Astrodome
8700 Kirby
Houston, TX 77054
(713) 799-9500

Los Angeles Dodgers
Dodger Stadium
1000 Elysian Park Ave.
Los Angeles, CA 90012
(213) 224-1500

Montreal Expos
Olympic Stadium
4545 Pierre-de-Coubertin
Montreal, Quebec
Canada HIV 3P2
(514) 253-3434

New York Mets
126 St. & Roosevelt Ave.
Flushing, NY 11368
(718) 507-6387

Philadelphia Phillies
Veterans Stadium
Broad & Pattison Aves.
Philadelphia, PA 19148
(215) 463-6000

Pittsburgh Pirates
Three Rrs Stadium
600 Stadium Circle
Pittsburgh, PA 15212
(412) 323-5000

St. Louis Cardinals
250 Stadium Plaza
St. Louis, MO 63102
(314) 421-4040

San Diego Padres
Jack Murphy Stadium
9449 Friars Rd.
San Diego, CA 92108
(619) 283-7294

San Francisco Giants
Candlestick Park
San Francisco, CA 94124
(415) 468-3700

NATIONAL HOCKEY LEAGUE

Boston Bruins
Boston Garden
150 Causeway St.
Boston, MA 02114
(617) 227-3206

Buffalo Sabres
Memorial Auditorium
140 Main Street
Buffalo, NY 14202
(716) 856-7300

Calgary Flames
Olympic Saddledome
Box 1540 Station M
Calgary, Canada AB T2P 3B9
(403) 261-0475

Chicago Blackhawks
1800 W. Madison
Chicago, IL 60612
(312) 733-5300

Detroit Red Wings
Joe Louis Arena
600 Civic Center Drive
Detroit, MI 48226
(313) 567-7333

Edmonton Oilers
Northlands Coliseum
7424—118 Avenue
Edmonton, Canada AB T5B 4M9
(403) 474-8561

Hartford Whalers
242 Trumbull St.
Hartford, CT 06013
(203) 728-3366

Los Angeles Kings
The Forum
P.O. Box 17013
Inglewood, CA 90308
(213) 419-3160

Minnesota North Stars
The Met Center
7901 Cedar Avenue S.
Bloomington, MN 55420
(612) 853-9333

Montreal Canadiens
The Forum
1414 Lambert Closse
Montreal, Canada Q H3H 1N2
(514) 932-2582

New Jersey Devils
Byrne Meadowlands
P.O. Box 504
East Rutherford, NJ 07073
(201) 935-6050

New York Islanders
Nassau Coliseum
Uniondale, NY 11553
(516) 794-4100

New York Rangers
4 Penn Plaza
New York, NY 10001
(212) 563-8000

Philadelphia Flyers
The Spectrum
Pattison Place
Philadelphia, PA
(215) 465-4500

Pittsburgh Penguins
Gate 7—Civic Arena
Pittsburgh, PA 15219
(412) 642-1800

Quebec Nodiques
Colisee de Quebec
2205 Ave de Colisse
Quebec, Canada Q GIL 4W7
(418) 529-8441

St. Louis Blues
5700 Oakland Avenue
St. Louis, MO 63110
(314) 781-5300

Toronto Maple Leafs
Maple Leaf Gardens
60 Carlton Street
Toronto, Ontario
M5B 1L1
(416) 977-1641

Vancouver Canucks
100 N. Renfrew St.
Vancouver, B.C.
V5K 3N7
(604) 254-5141

Washington Capitals
Capital Centre
Landover, MD 20785
(301) 386-7000

Winnipeg Jets
Winnipeg Arena
15-1430 Maroons Road
Winnipeg, Manitoba
R3G 0L5
(204) 772-9491

OLYMPIC SPORTS GOVERNING BODIES

National Archery Association
1750 East Boulder Street
Colorado Springs, CO 80909
(719) 578-4576

The Athletics Congress
P.O. Box 120
Indianapolis, IN 46206
(317) 261-0500

U.S. Badminton Association
501 West 6th Street
Papillion, NE 68046
(402) 592-7309

U.S. Baseball Federation
2160 Greenwood Avenue
Trenton, NJ 08609
(609) 586-2381

USA Basketball
1750 East Boulder Street
Colorado Springs, CO 80909
(719) 632-7687

U.S. Biathlon Association
P.O. Box 5515
Essex Junction, VT 05453
(802) 655-4524

Bobsled and Skeleton Federation
P.O. Box 828
Lake Placid, NY 12946
(518) 523-1842

USA Amateur Boxing Federation
1750 East Boulder Street
Colorado Springs, CO 80909
(719) 578-4506

U.S. Canoe and Kayak Team
Pan American Plaza, Suite 470
201 South Capitol Avenue
Indianapolis, IN 46225
(317) 237-5690

U.S. Cycling Federation
1750 East Boulder Street
Colorado Springs, CO 80909
(719) 578-4581

United States Diving, Inc.
Pan American Plaza, Suite 430
201 South Capitol Avenue
Indianapolis, IN 46225
(317) 237-5252

American Horse Shows Association
220 East 42nd Street, Suite 409
New York, NY 10017
(212) 972-2472

U.S. Fencing Association
1750 East Boulder Street
Colorado Springs, CO 80909
(719) 578-4511

Field Hockey Association of America (Men)
U.S. Field Hockey Association (Women)
1750 East Boulder Street
Colorado Springs, CO 80909
(719) 578-4587

Figure Skating Association
20 First Street
Colorado Springs, CO 80906
(719) 635-5200

U.S. Gymnastics Federation
Pan American Plaza, Suite 300
201 South Capitol Avenue
Indianapolis, IN 46225
(317) 237-5050

USA Hockey
2997 Broadmoor Valley Road
Colorado Springs, CO 80906
(719) 576-4990

United States Judo, Inc.
P.O. Box 10013
El Paso, TX 79991
(915) 565-8754

U.S. Luge Association
P.O. Box 651
Lake Placid, NY 12946
(518) 523-2071

U.S. Modern Pentathlon Association
P.O. Box 8178
San Antonio, TX 78208
(512) 246-3000

U.S. Rowing Association
Pan American Plaza, Suite 400
201 South Capitol Avenue
Indianapolis, IN 46225
(317) 237-5656

National Rifle Association
1600 Rhode Island Avenue, NW
Washington, D.C. 20036
(202) 828-6000

U.S. Ski Association
P.O. Box 100
Park City, UT 84060
(801) 649-9090

U.S. Soccer Federation
1750 East Boulder Street
Colorado Springs, CO 80909
(719) 578-4678

U.S. International Speedskating Association
1750 East Boulder Street
Colorado Springs, CO 80909
(719) 578-0661

U.S. Swimming, Inc.
1750 East Boulder Street
Colorado Springs, CO 80909
(719) 578-4578

U.S. Synchronized Swimming, Inc.
Pan American Plaza, Suite 510
201 South Capitol Avenue
Indianapolis, IN 46225
(317) 237-5700

U.S. Table Tennis Association
1750 East Boulder Street
Colorado Springs, CO 80909
(719) 578-4583

U.S. Team Handball Federation
1750 East Boulder Street
Colorado Springs, CO 80909
(719) 578-4582

U.S. Tennis Association
1212 Avenue of the Americas, 12th Floor
New York, NY 10036
(212) 302-3322

U.S. Volleyball Association
1750 East Boulder Street
Colorado Springs, CO 80909
(719) 578-4750

United States Water Polo
Pan American Plaza, Suite 520
201 South Capitol Avenue
Indianapolis, IN 46225
(317) 237-5599

U.S. Weightlifting Federation
1750 East Boulder Street
Colorado Springs, CO 80909
(719) 578-4508

USA Wrestling
225 South Academy Boulevard
Colorado Springs, CO 80910
(719) 597-8333

U.S. Yacht Racing Union
P.O. Box 209
Newport, RI 02840
(401) 849-5200

NATIONAL PARKS

The National Park Service administers the national parks through its main office in Washington D.C. and through regional offices located throughout the U.S. To obtain information about the national parks, you can certainly write to the main office. You'll receive more specific information if you write to the regional offices, and from there you can contact particular parks. The addresses below are listed according to the regional areas they serve, but the regional designation is not a part of the address. When you write, address your letter to the National Park Service, followed by the street address for the region you are interested in. For example, if you want to contact the Southeast Region, write to: National Park Service, 75 Spring Street SW, Atlanta, Ga. 30303.

National Office
P.O. Box 37127
Washington, DC 20013

North Atlantic Region
15 State Street
Boston, MA 02109

Mid-Atlantic Region
143 South Third Street
Philadelphia, PA 19106

National Capitol Region
1100 Ohio Drive SW
Washington, D.C. 20242

Southeast Region
75 Spring Street SW
Atlanta, GA 30303

Midwest Region
1709 Jackson Street
Omaha, NE 68102